S.O.S.
Social Skills in Our Schools

**A Social Skills Program for Children with
Pervasive Developmental Disorders, Including
High-Functioning Autism and Asperger Syndrome,
and Their Typical Peers**

S.O.S.
Social Skills in Our Schools

A Social Skills Program for Children with Pervasive Developmental Disorders, Including High-Functioning Autism and Asperger Syndrome, and Their Typical Peers

Michelle A. Dunn, Ph.D.

Foreword by Brenda Smith Myles

Autism Asperger Publishing Co.
P.O. Box 23173
Shawnee Mission, Kansas 66283-0173
www.asperger.net

© 2006 by Autism Asperger Publishing Co.
P.O. Box 23173
Shawnee Mission, Kansas 66283-0173
www.asperger.net

**Publisher's Cataloging-in-Publication
(Provided by Quality Books, Inc.)**

Dunn, Michelle A., 1959-
    S.O.S.— social skills in our schools : social skills
program for children with pervasive developmental
disorders, including high-functioning autism and
Asperger syndrome, and their typical peers / Michelle A.
Dunn.
      p. cm.
      SOS— social skills in our schools
      Includes bibliographical references.
      ISBN 1-931282-78-1
    LCCN 2005931098

    1. Autistic children—Rehabilitation. 2. Autistic
children—Education. 3. Social skills in children.
I. Title. II. Title: SOS— social skills in our schools
III. Title: Social skills in our schools

RJ506.A9D86 2005   618.92'8588203
                     QBI05-1397

This book is designed in Futura and Churchward
Printed in the United States of America

ACKNOWLEDGMENTS

This program was developed in response to the expressed needs of two school districts in New York State – Roslyn Union Free School District and Eastchester School District. Staff in both districts made significant contributions to this program through their feedback as they delivered the curriculum. Some contributed materials and specific ideas for activities. Credit is given for those contributions throughout this book.

I would like to gratefully acknowledge the significant contributions of:

Sheryl Chuzmir   Susan Levine

Felice Silverman   Barbara Wygoda

*This book is dedicated to all of the children
with PDD and their families who have
participated in the S.O.S. program.*

Foreword

Social skills challenges are complex and, therefore, cannot be remediated with piecemeal and erratically scheduled lessons. In addition, social skills instruction must go beyond teaching appropriate behaviors and manners to addressing the myriad deficits that underlie social problems. Michelle Dunn understands this – perhaps more than anyone I have known. Dr. Dunn is a rare individual – a scholar and practitioner. Her book, *S.O.S.: Social Skills in Our Schools*, is a gift to individuals with pervasive developmental disorders (PDD), their neurotypical peers, their teachers and parents. Field-tested for a number of years, this curriculum is backed by both research in effectively teaching social skills and by practice.

This program is not for the teacher or parent who wishes to occasionally teach a social skills lesson. It was developed for schools that wish to make a serious commitment to helping children with high-functioning autism (HFA), Asperger Syndrome (AS), and other PDDs successfully and enjoyably interact with others at school, at home, and in the community. The program is well conceptualized and does things that no other curriculum has attempted. For example, the curriculum has built-in booster lessons, because Dunn recognizes that our children require more than one presentation of material and need reminders. It includes pull-out lessons for children with PDDs, recognizing that sometimes our children and youth need specialized instruction and practice to understand and begin to use a skill. The S.O.S. program also addresses the all-important topic of generalization by including social skills lessons for *all* students in the general education classroom. While intended to foster understanding and friendships between students with and without PDD, these lessons also teach general education peers social skills – something almost all children need.

And it doesn't stop there. This comprehensive social skills program also incorporates (a) a strong peer mentoring program; (b) a parent training component; (c) "homework" lessons that offer parents and children opportunities to explore social skills together in a meaningful and fun way; and (d) training for the S.O.S. supervisor – the individual who is carrying out the program.

When I was asked to write the foreword for this book, I was very honored and saw this as a relatively simple task, because I am very familiar with Michelle Dunn's work, including this curriculum. However, writing this review was a challenge. I started several times to identify and discuss the components of social skills training, but Dunn has provided the reader with this information in a very user-friendly format. I also wanted to discuss what we as researchers have identified as important components, but again this empirical evidence is very clearly presented. In short, the book discusses all salient issues and ideas that belong in a social skills curriculum. Ideas that work – ideas that have been tested and modified to ensure that they match the needs of our children.

This curriculum is wonderful in its scope and practical nature, and as a professor I will use it to teach my graduate students how to implement social skills programs in schools. In addition, I will refer them to Dr. Dunn as they continue to develop their skills. I cannot do this book justice in a few brief paragraphs. S.O.S. is a curriculum that stands by itself. It can truly make a meaningful difference in the lives of children and youth with HFA, AS, and other PDDs and those who teach, care for, and interact with them.

– Brenda Smith Myles, Ph.D., associate professor, the University of Kansas

Author and co-author of numerous publications, Myles' recent books include
The Hidden Curriculum: Practical Solutions for Understanding Unstated Rules in Social Situations,
Asperger Syndrome and Adolescence: Practical Solutions for School Success,
Asperger Syndrome and Sensory Issues: Practical Solutions for Making Sense of the World and
*Asperger Syndrome and Difficult Moments: Practical Solutions for Tantrums, Rage, and Meltdowns –
New Revised and Expanded Edition*

Table of Contents

S.O.S. – Social Skills in Our Schools

Introduction

S.O.S. – Social Skills in Our Schools – is a comprehensive social skills curriculum for verbal children with pervasive developmental disorders (PDD), including high-functioning autism and Asperger Syndrome, in grades 1 through 6 and their typical peers.

Language and occupational therapies that address communication, auditory processing, motor, and some organizational issues are typically available as ancillary services in schools. However, most schools at this time do not provide social skills intervention by specially trained staff to their students with PDD, despite the often serious deficits these children exhibit.

Simply exposing children with PDD to typically developing children in school does little to develop social skills (Pierce & Schreibman, 1997). They do not learn appropriate social interaction by "osmosis." The S.O.S. program addresses this issue head-on through its dual purpose: (a) to develop appropriate social skills in high-functioning, verbal children with PDD and (b) to foster understanding and tolerance of individual differences, a stronger sense of fairness, and increased social initiations toward children with differences by typical children in the same general education settings.

Operating on a schoolwide basis, the program consists of four major components:

- pull-out social skills lessons for children with PDD

- social skills lessons in the classroom for all children (intended to develop tolerance and fairness and foster initiations to the children with PDD)

- peer mentoring

- parent training

The curriculum is presented in the school setting over the course of two academic years. Participating children may be fully included in the general education classroom or be enrolled in partially or fully self-contained classes. The program is carried out by school staff with training and supervision offered by an autism expert with special training in the the S.O.S. program (see page 22 for information on obtaining S.O.S. school supervisor certification). The intention is to empower the staff to address the needs of their students with PDD through training and support.

In the following we will outline the most salient characteristics of pervasive developmental disorders with an emphasis on social skills deficits. This will be followed by a review of current social skills intervention programs for children with PDD.

Pervasive Developmental Disorders (PDDs)

The PDDs, which include autism, Asperger Syndrome, and PDD-not otherwise specified, are diagnosed based on a combination of deficits in the areas of socialization, communication, and behavior, involving rigidity, perseveration, and preoccupations. A broad range of impairment is observed in each of these three dimensions. The disorders are not defined by overall cognitive level. Thus, intelligence ranges from the severely challenged to individuals in the very superior range with specific cognitive deficits in attention, organization, and planning. Due to these characteristics, major areas requiring intervention include socialization, communication, motor function, planning and organization, auditory and other sensory issues, perseveration, preoccupation, and rigidity.

Social Skills Deficits in Children with PDD

Teacher ratings and results of standardized measures of social skills confirm impaired socialization as the hallmark of children on the autism spectrum. Specifically, children with autism spectrum disorders initiate and are engaged in interactions less, do not automatically attend to relevant social cues (Stainback & Stainback, 1984), and demonstrate more non-social behaviors than typical peers (Koegel, Koegel, Frea, & Fredeen, 2001; McConnell, 2002). Children with PDD have great difficulty establishing reciprocal social relationships. They have atypical eye contact. They may fail to make eye contact or they may not use it to guide turn taking during social interaction. Further, they do not direct facial expressions to others in the typical way and have limited joint attention (i.e., the ability to focus on a common object or event).

As a result, these children have limited play skills and have great difficulty sustaining social interaction in play or conversation. They rarely initiate social interaction in an appropriate way with peers, and their typical peers' confusion about how to respond often rapidly terminates a social interaction that has begun. Some children on the autism spectrum are over-initiators while others are passive, quiet under-initiators. Some under-initiators are *socially isolated* and do not respond well to social approaches from others. Yet others are *socially remote* in that they do not initiate interaction but respond if approached.

However, more often than not verbal children with PDD are socially motivated and want to initiate, but they do not know how to appropriately make social contact or sustain an interaction. These children have trouble with the back and forth of playground play and conversation, and perseverative behaviors and preoccupations interfere with interaction. For example, some children with PDD are hyper-verbal and talk endlessly about their own topics even though their peers are not interested. Some children make social approaches by perseveratively chasing and touching other children on the playground. Further, they often have trouble modulating their silliness when having fun, and consequently get carried away. Modulation of all emotions is difficult for them. Motives, intentions, and emotions of peers are elusive (Cardon, 2004).

Even high-functioning children with PDD demonstrate impairment in verbal and nonverbal communication, and many report having fewer friends, less satisfying relations, and being lonelier than their typical peers (Bauminger & Kasari, 2000). Specifically, they have difficulty interpreting tone of voice, gestures, and body posture (Volkmar & Klin, 1998).

Without intervention, many otherwise socially motivated children with PDD are left on the social periphery, and even if they develop better social skills, they continue to be rejected due to the reputation they have established.

The most important educational goals for these children are to develop social and communicative competence. It is especially important that they have an opportunity to develop these skills as they are strongly related to later coping in adolescence and adulthood. That is, social skills deficits, just like communication or motor impairment, present a significant impediment to learning and a successful, productive adulthood. Even many very high-functioning individuals with PDD fail to find employment commensurate with their intellect or are unable to maintain a job due to impaired social skills (Rumsey & Hamburger, 1988). Further, many individuals with PDD become depressed due to greater awareness of their social skills deficits and failure to develop relationships.

**MAJOR SOCIAL SKILLS CHARACTERISTICS
IN CHILDREN WITH PDD**

- Impaired verbal and nonverbal pragmatics
- Poor joint attention
- Poor attention to social cues
- Initiating and engaging less or inappropriately in social interaction
- Limited reciprocity
- Perseveration and preoccupations
- Problems with behavioral/emotional modulation

Social Skills Interventions for Children with PDD

For children with PDD, social skills are an educational issue, not solely a parental responsibility. Schools are the primary social venue for children, especially those with PDD. However, the majority of schools have no systematic, developmental approach to fostering social skills in children. Even when schools are motivated to include social skills in the curriculum, it can be difficult to fit such programs into the schedule. Further, community organizations that foster the development of social skills in typical children, such as Scouting and other youth groups, are usually not equipped to support children with PDD.

In an effort to improve socialization, schools place many high-functioning, and even some low-functioning, children with PDD in general education classrooms. As a result, classroom teachers are responsible for an increasingly diverse population of students. However, these general education teachers typically have little training in how to deal with the behaviors of children with PDD (e.g., perseveration, impaired ability to deal with transitions, difficulty with emotional modulation) as well as with their cognitive and language needs. And even when these children are accompanied by individual assistants or paraeducators, these aides often have little training or familiarity with the students' needs.

In general, parents prefer inclusion settings for their children once they reach school age (Kasari, Freeman, Bauminger, & Alkin, 1999). Some professionals advocate for a general education setting based on the assumptions of consequent improvements of the child's social behavior and other children's acceptance of peers with differences just through exposure (Villa & Thousand, 1995). However, neither assumption bears out. Simply placing a child with PDD in a general education classroom does little to build social skills in that child or acceptance in his or her typical peers (Burack, Root, & Zigler, 1997). More direct social skills interventions must be put in place.

Improvement in social skills is critical to the long-term outcome of individuals with PDD (Matson & Swiezy, 1994; Schopler & Mesibov, 1983). Social skills intervention is an essential and necessary part of any comprehensive program for children with PDD. Intervention should begin early, and continued support should be provided throughout school and later life. Unlike language and motor skills where a certain level of competence once achieved generally allows a person to succeed, social skills are a moving target. That is, for every person, each stage of development presents new social challenges and requires direct instruction to meet them.

There are two major classes of social skills intervention: adult-mediated and peer-mediated.

Adult-Mediated Interventions

A variety of methods have been used in adult-mediated social skills intervention with varying success. Some interventions were developed specifically for working with children with PDD; others were not, but may be adapted for this purpose. Some address circumscribed goals such as developing social communication through scripting language on cards (McClannahan & Krantz 1999) or developing social understanding (through photos and drawings) and pretend play (Howlin, Baron-Cohen, & Hadwin, 1999). Others seek to teach and provide practice in implementing a wide range of social rules and strategies (Attwood, 2003; Baker, 2003; Duke, Nowicki, & Martin, 1996;

Gajewski, Hirn, & Mayo, 1993, 1994; Garcia-Winner, 2003; Gutstein & Sheely, 2002; McAfee, 2001; McGinnis & Goldstein, 1997; Moyes & Moreno, 2001; Myles & Southwick, 2005).

Theory of mind. Some interventions attempt to address what some researchers see as the core underlying deficit in PDD, "theory of mind" the ability to infer others' thoughts and predict others' actions (Howlin et al., 1999). For example, Ozonoff and Miller (1995) trained "theory of mind" in a small group of children with autism. Their approach was partially successful. After treatment they noted improvements in "theory of mind" tasks (false belief tasks), but the improvements were not related to improved social interaction as demonstrated on parent and teacher ratings of social competence. That is, although the children appeared to learn what they were directly taught, they did not generalize those skills to other environments.

Social autopsies. Other adult-mediated interventions address social problem solving. One example is LaVoie's social autopsies (Bieber, 1994). This approach teaches children to evaluate cause-and-effect relationships between their social behaviors and the positive and negative reactions they receive from others. Social situations are discussed with an adult after the fact to help children identify alternate solutions to the social problem, and a plan is made to avoid the mistake in the future.

Social Stories™. Other popular methods for conveying information and teaching children with PDD about social behavior include Social Stories and comic strip conversations. A Social Story (Gray, 1994b) is a brief story used to explain social rules and concepts. For example, books of Social Stories teach children behaviors such as playing a game, riding the school bus, and making transitions. Individual Social Stories may also be written for a given child based on the child's needs and characteristics. Stories are written in a matter-of-fact way and present information so it is easily understood (it may include pictures and icons and should include language that is developmentally appropriate). Gray's Social Stories include specific sentences that provide information about the child, setting, action, and feelings of others.

Comic strip conversations. Comic strip conversations (Gray, 1994a) are designed to help children with PDD understand social and communicative interactions using simple stick figure drawings of people conversing. Comic strip conversations are particularly beneficial for children with PDD, who are better at processing concrete visual information than auditory information, because they turn fleeting, auditory information into a visual referent that remains present and stable until processed.

Videotaping. Another way to present and teach social information is through the use of videotapes (Charlop & Milstein, 1989; Charlop-Christy & Daneshvar, 2003; Charlop-Christy, Le, & Freeman, 2000). Videotaped self-modeling (Buggey, 1999) allows the child to look at his own behavior as an outside observer. It can take several forms, including positive self-review (PSR) and video feed-forward (Dowrick, 1999).

Both PSR and video feed-forward involve taping the child and then editing out inappropriate instances of a target behavior so that the child sees himself implementing the behavior in only an appropriate way – getting it right. PSR shows a single behavior, whereas video feed-forward focuses on chaining together behaviors that the child already is able to execute in isolation but cannot yet sequence. Videotaping can also facilitate social autopsies. In this approach children (a) view videotaped interaction with an adult; (b) discuss situations that went poorly or well and others' reactions, consequences, or alternative behaviors; and (c) develop a plan for next time.

Children with PDD typically cannot recognize inappropriate behavior when they produce it. They are better able to see it when they can observe themselves from outside. Rather than telling the child how to implement a skill, the video format immediately shows both mistakes and successful implementation of a skill. Overall, the use of videotapes in social skills intervention takes advantage of a common strength in concrete visual processing and the attraction that many children with PDD have for videotapes, resulting in better attention to the information being presented. Finally, it allows the children to look again and again at their behavior, learn the appropriate behavior and, in some cases, with the support of an adult, understand how it functions for them.

Types of groups. Adult-mediated interventions take place in either individual or group sessions, ranging in membership and level of structure. For example, social skills groups may be made up exclusively of children on the spectrum or may include typically developing peers as well (Kamps et al., 1992). While many groups use the structured interventions discussed in this section, some are simply play sessions in a safe environment, where the teacher or other adult sometimes intervenes to increase interaction or trouble-shoot. Unfortunately, the latter approach does not acknowledge the attentional style of children with autism spectrum disorders. Instead, a cognitive-behavioral approach involving direct teaching of social rules and strategies, practice, and, later on, problem solving is required.

**ADULT-MEDIATED SOCIAL SKILLS
INTERVENTION METHODS**

- Group or individual sessions
- Scripting language
- Learning, teaching, and practicing social rules
- Teaching of "theory of mind"
- Social problem solving through social autopsies
- Social Stories™
- Comic strip conversations
- Videotaped self-modeling

Peer-Mediated Approaches

As the name implies, peer-mediated approaches provide social skills support and/or instruction through typical peers (Rogers, 2000). Sometimes the peers are older, at other times they are the same age as the target children. Of the two, same-age peers have been found to be more effective (Lord & Hopkins, 1986). Sometimes the peers are specifically trained; at other times they are not. However, trained peers produce greater results.

There are three major types of peer-mediated intervention: (a) peers are simply told to play with the child with PDD; (b) peers prompt and reinforce the child with PDD for a target social behavior; and (c) peers are told to initiate social interactions with the child with PDD. With all three types some increase in social behavior has been observed among children with PDD, but prompting and initiations by peers are more effective than proximity alone (Odom & Strain, 1984).

In some cases typical peers interact with children with PDD in the context of social skills groups (Kamps et al., 1992); in others, they serve as academic tutors (Kamps, Barbetta, Leonard, & Delquadri, 1994) or as support during unstructured times of the day in school (Haring & Breen, 1992).

Typical peers serving as tutors or mentors can increase the social and communication interaction of children with PDD. For example, training typical peers to use an augmentative communication system (Kamps, Potucek, Lopez, Kravits, & Kemmerer, 1997) with children with PDD resulted in neurotypical peers becoming more accepting of children with PDD and interacting with them more. Similarly, teaching typical peers to use pivotal response training techniques, such as encouraging attention, turn taking, and conversation; modeling appropriate social behavior; giving the child with PDD choices; and reinforcement (Pierce & Schreibman, 1997), was related to increases in language and social skills, including joint attention. Not surprisingly, to ensure the most effective generalization, it is best to have multiple peers as partners for children with PDD (Belchic & Harris, 1994; Pierce & Schreibman, 1997).

In some programs like Circle of Friends, peers meet on a regular basis with a supervisor/facilitator and monitor their own interactions with the children with PDD (Haring & Breen, 1992; Sainato, Goldstein, & Strain, 1992). If the interactions of typical peers are not monitored, the frequency of initiations with their peers with PDD tends to drop (Odom & Watts, 1991).

PEER-MEDIATED SOCIAL SKILLS INTERVENTION METHODS

- Group or individual sessions
- Same-age peers (best)
- Trained peers (best)
- Peer academic tutoring
- Circle of Friends
- Peer proximity
- Peer initiating
- Peer prompting and reinforcing

Characteristics of Effective Social Skills Interventions

Little research has evaluated the effectiveness of social skills intervention for school-age children with PDD, especially those who are higher functioning (Marriage, Gordon, & Brand, 1995). Most studies have focused on social skills training for lower-functioning children (e.g., Wolfberg & Schuler, 1993) or adolescents and adults with autism (Mesibov, 1984).

As already discussed, many studies support the clinical impression of improvements in at least some aspect of social behavior through both adult-mediated and peer-mediated interventions. However, most of these studies involved few subjects and employed single-subject designs. Individually, they do not provide insight into the general characteristics of effective social skills intervention.

In their study *Improving Efficacy of Social Skills Interventions*, Gresham, Sugai, and Horner (2001) presented a meta-analysis of social skills intervention studies completed in an attempt to establish the features of social skills interventions that make them effective. Specifically, they evaluated the studies with regard to acquisition (how effectively the children initially learned the skills); generalization (whether skills were demonstrated across different settings); and maintenance (whether skills were maintained after a period of time). They concluded that direct teaching of skills, modeling, coaching, and reinforcement are necessary components of an effective intervention. This is consistent with Mesibov's (1984) qualitative data suggesting that highly verbal adolescents with autism benefited from an approach involving modeling, coaching, and role-play aimed at developing communication, peer interaction, and self-esteem.

Gresham et al. (2001) indicated that weaknesses of current social skills interventions include failure to tailor the intervention to the type of social deficit demonstrated (acquisition, performance, fluency), limited frequency and intensity of the intervention, and an attempt to teach too many skills at once or just one skill for a short period. In addition, these authors noted that most approaches demonstrate poor generalization and maintenance of skills.

Marriage et al. (1995) found that even when an intervention tried to promote generalization through changes in group leader and setting (room and building), skills did not generalize to school, home, and the community. It appears that children with PDD learn skills in association with the specific environment in which they are taught. Therefore, for skills to be generalized to all environments, they must be taught/reinforced in all environments.

The next chapter will introduce *S.O.S. – Social Skills in Our Schools* and show how the program responds to all the major criticisms of other current approaches to social skills intervention.

S.O.S.:
A SOCIAL SKILLS INTERVENTION MODEL FOR SCHOOLS

So what type of social skills intervention makes sense for high-functioning children with PDD? To develop peer interaction skills, social skills training must happen in school, the setting in which children spend the most time with their peers. Further, as with all interventions for children with PDD, the form social skills intervention takes should be guided by the child's neuropsychological profile of cognitive and linguistic strengths and weaknesses.

The S.O.S. program takes research, clinical experience, and the characteristics of children with PDD into account, with an emphasis on children's strengths. Briefly, the structure and methods used in the S.O.S. program are driven by the neuropsychological profiles of children with PDD. The idea is to emphasize the child's processing strengths and use them to improve or compensate for processing weaknesses.

According to Minshew, Goldstein, and Siegel (1997), high-functioning individuals on the autism spectrum, with the exception of some individuals with Asperger Syndrome, demonstrate relative strengths in visual perception, visual spatial skills, and visual information processing. Relative weaknesses are observed in auditory and language processing. All individuals with diagnoses on the spectrum have relative strengths in simple language processing, simple auditory and visual memory, and concrete information processing. Weaknesses are demonstrated in complex language and memory, organization and planning, as well as in abstract information processing. For example, children with PDD have difficulty allocating attention to the most important information in the environment and do not automatically shift their attention when needed, even when they are cued to do so. Therefore, to ensure they learn, it is necessary to focus the children's attention on goals and expectations. *S.O.S. does this through direct teaching.*

1. The children are told exactly what it is they are expected to pay attention to and learn in each lesson.

2. As they observe social behaviors modeled by their peers or adult teachers, they are explicitly told what to attend to.

3. Then they role-play exactly what they have been taught, and the parents, who are aware of the content of every lesson, practice with the children at home.

Further, to be effective the interventions should acknowledge the child's learning style and employ the child's cognitive and linguistic strengths to teach her to overcome or compensate for social deficits. Children with PDD are stronger at concrete, visual information processing. Rote memory for simple auditory and visual information is typically a relative strength. Behaviors and language are frequently memorized with repeated exposure to the information before those behaviors or language are understood. Therefore, most children with PDD effectively memorize social scripts and coping behaviors, and even perform these behaviors in other environments when prompted and reinforced, but they usually only understand the meaning and function of these behaviors later. *The S.O.S. program uses numerous concrete, visual referents and takes advantage of rote memory for initial acquisition, later teaching what the behavior means for the child and how it works.*

Social skills intervention must also be guided by knowledge of a child's social skills deficit profile. Social skills impairment in children with PDD primarily involves acquisition, performance, and/or fluency deficits. Social skills intervention should not only be focused on helping the child to acquire social skills, but must encourage performance and, ultimately, fluency in all environments. A teacher with awareness of these types of social skills deficits can determine, through observation, whether a given child needs more emphasis on (a) learning rules for appropriate social behavior, (b) implementing social rules she already knows, or (c) using social skills automatically and fluently. *The S.O.S. program addresses social skills deficits in all three areas.*

Initial acquisition of specific social skills is fostered through direct teaching, modeling, coaching, and role-play. Performance of the skills in all environments is subsequently developed through prompting and reinforcement by peers, teachers, and parents and by helping the children to understand the consequences of their actions. Finally, fluency in independent implementation of skills is addressed through rehearsal during the sessions in which the skills are taught as well as prompted practice in ecologically valid situations on a daily basis (the classroom, the playground, at home, with peers and with adults). Throughout, the program effectively helps children to generalize their newly learned skills by providing a socially accepting environment and through prompting and reinforcement in all settings.

The skills in the S.O.S. curriculum are taught over two academic years. In the first year, all the social rules in the curriculum are scripted. In the second year, repetition of the curriculum develops fluency in implementing the skills and develops an understanding of how the behavior functions for the child. This is because it cannot be assumed that just because a child can articulate a script he knows when, how, or why to use it or that he will even attempt to use it. *Along with developing performance and fluency, the S.O.S. program includes an emphasis on generalization and maintenance of skills.*

Staff and Parent Training

To start successful implementation of the S.O.S. program, school staff (including general education teachers, language pathologists, guidance counselors, resource room teachers, self-contained classroom teachers, school psychologists, and any other staff members who are interested) and the parents of children with PDD receive training in PDD and in the S.O.S social skills intervention from an autism expert, preferable someone certified in the S.O.S program. The training for staff typically occurs as a two-day workshop. School staff under the supervision of the S.O.S. expert then carries out this program. (See page 22 for information regarding obtaining certification as an S.O.S. school supervisor.)

Separate training is also conducted for parents. The mentor supervisor holds one meeting with the parents of the mentors in the fall once mentors have been selected. Further, the certified S.O.S. supervisor meets with the parents of the children with PDD on a bi-monthly basis during the school year (five times). (See pages 25-26 for further information about training for both staff and parents. See also Parent Training, pages 225-230.)

Maintenance and Generalization

Since children with PDD tend to learn skills in association with the specific environment in which they are taught, skills are taught and reinforced in all environments. Specifically, in the S.O.S. program, socialization is reinforced in the classroom through the teacher and typical peers, who are supported in initiating interactions with their peers with PDD. Further, skills are reinforced during recess and lunch by trained peer mentors, and at home by the parents (who, as mentioned above, receive training in separate bi-monthly sessions). The program combines adult- and peer-mediated interventions. Adult-mediated intervention, delivered in small groups comprised of children with PDD, provides direct instruction in social rules, strategies, and problem solving. In addition, peer-mediated interventions are delivered in all classrooms and by a smaller group of trained peer mentors during lunch and recess. Finally, incidental instruction in natural contexts and direct instruction is provided by the trained peer mentors.

This combined approach, where all members of the social network, including peers and staff, are educated, encourages maintenance and generalization of newly learned social skills in the children with PDD and addresses socialization in the entire school community.

Dual Purpose

As mentioned, the S.O.S. program has a dual purpose: (a) developing appropriate social skills in high-functioning, verbal children with PDD and (b) fostering in typical children understanding of individual differences, broader tolerance, and a stronger sense of fairness, as well as the initiative to act on what they understand and believe. Just as the major goal for the children with PDD is to replace inappropriate behaviors with appropriate ones, so it is for the children with typical development.

This type of intervention program benefits both the children with PDD and their typically developing peers, who demonstrate increased self-esteem, connectedness to community, and achievement test scores (Twemlow et al., 2001) as a result of their involvement in peer mentoring. High self-esteem and firm connections to peers, family, and the school community are associated with a significant reduction in risky behaviors as a child grows up. Further, peer mentoring is important for the mentors in that it supports the idea that one person can effect change and that it is better to act on something in which you believe than just talking about it. Thus, there is justification for using a peer-mediated approach to social skills intervention not only for children with PDD but also for the typical peers who participate in such a program.

Program Effectiveness

A pilot study of the S.O.S. program was run in the first year of its implementation (Dunn, submitted for publication) to investigate its effectiveness. Thirty children with high-functioning autism – by the combined criteria of the Autism Diagnostic Observational Scale (ADOS; Lord et al., 2000) and clinical diagnosis (including history) – were enrolled. Half of the students received the S.O.S. intervention and half did not. All children continued to receive their typical ancillary services. The groups were matched by chronological age and IQ.

Results of time sampling of inappropriate and appropriate social initiations in both structured and unstructured situations indicated that after five months, nearly all children in the treatment and non-treatment groups showed a decrease in inappropriate social initiations. However, children receiving the S.O.S. program also demonstrated an increase in appropriate social initiations above what was seen with typical school services. Children in the non-treatment group were subsequently enrolled in the S.O.S. program. After five months they too showed a significant increase in appropriate social initiations.

Components of the S.O.S. Program

The S.O.S. model for social skills intervention is the original creation of the author as are most of the lessons. However, some lessons are based on or drawn from other excellent social skills and character education curricula (e.g., Baker, 2003; Gajewski et al., 1993, 1994; Lewis, 1998), as indicated where appropriate. The S.O.S. program employs multiple methods, both adult- and peer-mediated, in the school environment to foster fluency and generalization to all settings.

The four major components of the S.O.S. program are as follows:

- Pull-out sessions to teach social rules and provide practice opportunities to children with PDD

- Social skills lessons in the classroom

- Peer mentoring

- Parent involvement

Pull-Out Sessions: Teaching Social Skills to Children with PDD

Social skills lessons are usually taught to children with PDD in weekly social skills groups of no more than six children. In some instances, individual sessions are necessary as outlined below.

Group vs. Individual Session

The decision as to whether a child belongs in a social skills group or needs individual sessions depends on several factors:

- Does the child have some ability to inhibit behavior when necessary and cued to do so? Can the child follow instructions in a group? Can the child wait?

- Does the child attend to other children and demonstrate joint attention at least some of the time?

- Does the child have some awareness of his social skills difficulties? Is he socially motivated to improve his relationships? (Children with higher intellectual capability tend to have better awareness of their social deficits; Capps, Sigman, & Yirmiya, 1995; and are able to use cognitive social scripts effectively; Volden & Johnston, 1999.)

If the answer to these questions is no, the child should start in individual sessions until she has developed the prerequisite rudimentary abilities. If the answer to the questions is yes, the child is likely to benefit from group sessions, with one caveat – even if the child is cognitively, linguistically, and behaviorally ready, inclusion in a group also depends on the child's locus of control.

Does the child have an exclusively external locus of control? Specifically, does he blame others (parents, teachers, other students) for his difficulties? Before a child can engage in social skills intervention or join a group, he must come to some understanding that he is responsible for his behavior and can make his social situation better by changing certain behaviors. He must also accept that social skills group may help bring about such change.

It is often relatively easy to help a younger child with an external locus of control to understand this sense of control and responsibility, but it can pose difficulties for an older child who previously has had no sense of responsibility for his successes or failures. This is especially true if the child has been bullied, as this seems to be proof positive that others are responsible for the child's anger and inappropriate behaviors. It is important for this child to open himself to the possibility that he can change how others respond to him by learning and implementing new social skills. In the individual sessions leading up to membership in a social skills group, a child with this perspective needs help understanding that he chooses his own behavior (not the behavior of others) and that his behavior leads to consequences that are not of his choosing but are generally predictable. If he wants to change the consequences, he has to change his behavior.

Social skills intervention – whether in individual or group sessions – should begin as soon as a child's diagnosis is clear. Without early intervention a child with PDD is likely to establish a negative reputation. In that case the focus of intervention would not only involve instruction in social rules but would also stress inhibiting social interaction and inappropriate behaviors ("lying low") until better skills are developed and the negative reputation diminishes (Bierman, 1989). In addition, a child who needs to improve his reputation must be helped by peer-mediated approaches, which tend to increase peer acceptance.

As mentioned, most often the S.O.S. lessons are taught in groups. A group contains no more than six children with PDD grouped by language level (as assessed through standardized testing of expressive, and particularly receptive, language). The approach in these lessons is cognitive behavioral and adult-mediated. The major aim is to teach children to replace their inappropriate social behaviors with appropriate ones. While a structured school setting can be effective in reducing inappropriate behaviors, instruction in social rules increases appropriate behaviors.

Social rules and strategies are taught through direct instruction, modeling, and structured role-plays. Specifically, rules are made explicit and drilled, and the children write out the rules in their social skills notebook (see pages 58-59). Role-plays by the adult are used to demonstrate inappropriate social skills and subsequently model appropriate alternatives. Further, role-plays by children with PDD are used to practice the correct implementation of social rules and strategies. Plenty of rote practice is provided. Finally, homework to reinforce the rule at home is distributed and explained at the end of each session. Other methods that may be used are discussed under adult-mediated interventions (pages 4-6).

Five classes of goals are covered in the S.O.S. pull-outs: modulation of behavior and emotional responses; learning social rules; understanding the main idea in language/conversation and social situations and responding in an organized way with a focus on the main idea; reduction of perseverations and preoccupations; and developing insight. Each of these will be further discussed below.

1. Modulation of Behavior and Emotional Responses

Emotional and behavioral modulation is developed first through teaching a script for self-calming/stopping. The script must be practiced repeatedly "out of the heat of the moment" for the child to have any chance of using the strategy when he begins to lose control. Both the parents and the child must understand that this script will only work if the child is not too far out of control. Once out-of-control behavior has reached a critical point, an adult must intervene to help the child stop. The child will not be able to do it himself. However, with practice of the stopping strategy, the child's critical threshold will increase and out-of-control behavior will become less frequent.

The script is practiced so the child will be better able to use it when cued, thereby gaining more self-control. In particular, the script is practiced repeatedly in situations that elicit silliness, mild anxiety, anger, or engagement in preoccupations or perseverative behavior. Later the child is taught about the specific situations that elicit strong emotions or perseverative behaviors so that he can learn to anticipate the feelings he will experience and how to manage them before they get out of hand.

An important general goal is helping the child to feel responsible for himself, his belongings, and his own improvements and difficulties. A sense of responsibility in combination with successfully achieving goals increases self-esteem and motivation as well as self-control. This goal is the focus of some of the social skills lessons. Parents can help by giving their child responsibilities at home.

2. Learning Social Rules

A variety of social rules are addressed in the S.O.S. pull-out sessions. Examples include appropriate interpretation and generation/self-monitoring of body language (i.e., eye contact, gaze, facial expressions and gestures, tone and volume of voice) and prosody (rhythm, rate and melody of speech); beginning and maintaining interactions; making and maintaining friends; and rules for playing games that are common among the child's peers.

A special group of social skills rules falls under the heading of conversational skills. Work on conversational skills involves developing an understanding of the four parts of conversation (greeting, small talk, main point, closing); topic identification and maintenance; ability to continue topics initiated by others with an emphasis on the range of topics common to same-age peers; strategies for appropriately shifting topic; and bridging to a new topic.

Children with PDD must also ultimately be directly taught about humor, figurative language, idioms, irony, sarcasm, and metaphor. In addition, these children require direct instruction in interpretation of cause and effect and in drawing inferences.

3. Understanding the Main Idea

Children with PDD regularly process and remember details but have trouble seeing the forest for the trees. The S.O.S. program places an emphasis on teaching the children to identify the main idea of language/conversation or a social situation. Appropriate initiations in conversation or play and topic maintenance are impossible if one cannot identify the topic. How to formulate and organize a coherent narrative is addressed as well. Here the child is not given specific language scripts but the hierarchic organization of language is scripted. A concrete visually based approach, graphic organizers, is the method of choice given the neuropsychological profile of the majority of children with PDD. The diagram below is an example of a graphic organizer used to describe an event. Details of how to use graphic organizers for conversation, producing a narrative, understanding another's narrative, and understanding social situations are provided in the S.O.S. curriculum.

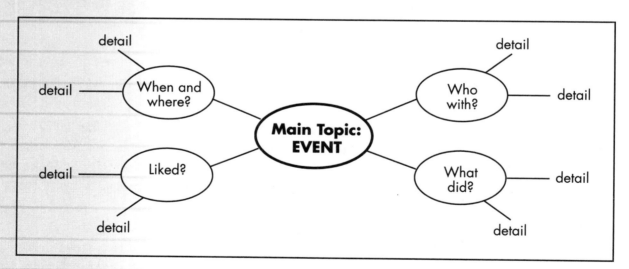

4. Reduction of Perseverations and Preoccupations

Preoccupations and perseverative behaviors are addressed by teaching competing appropriate behaviors and by providing a specific, limited time and place in which the child can engage in preoccupations and repetitive behaviors.

5. Developing Insight

Insight is developed in two ways. Lessons are taught that focus on developing awareness of the impact of the child's behavior on others, their reactions to him, and other consequences. This is done through (a) books about fictional characters who brag, are overactive, or mean; and (b) Personal Stories.

Each week the parent and child fill in a Personal Story graphic organizer about a social situation that occurs, good or bad (see page 70). One branch of the organizer contains the details of what happened, another lists the details of the consequences for the child, and the third contains details about what the child should do next time.

For children who are relatively new to social skills intervention, the branch on the graphic organizer about what to do next time is filled in by the parent and/or teacher as a social rule to be memorized. With further development, the child is asked to problem solve what the rule should be. "Good" stories are just as important as stories about inappropriate behavior. For example, if a child successfully uses his script for stopping when he is beginning to become over-anxious about schoolwork, the consequences would be that everyone was proud of him, he felt good about himself, and he got his work done. The answer to the question what he should do differently the next time is "nothing."

In addition to developing insight into the cause-and-effect relationships of behaviors and consequences, Personal Stories make the social skills trainer aware of problem situations that repeatedly occur in the child's life, teach social rules that may not be part of the standard developmentally ordered S.O.S. curriculum, develop problem-solving skills, and through "good" stories, reinforce appropriate implementation of social rules.

Facilitating Success

Lots of practice is necessary to make the newly acquired behaviors more potent than the old, inappropriate, automatic ones – especially in stressful situations. For many adults, the best example of this is when we drive a car. We know all the socially appropriate behaviors but in a stressful situation, as when someone cuts us off in traffic, inappropriate behaviors/language automatically tend to come out. Appropriate behaviors must be very potent to compete with automatic inappropriate ones.

In addition to teaching a set of specific social rules, it is important to individualize instruction for each child based on recurring difficulties. This may be accomplished by asking parents and classroom teachers to provide lists of what they see as the top-three behavioral/social goals for a given child. In addition, Personal Stories (described under Developing Insight) can provide a great deal of information about situations that recur at home so intervention can be individualized to address them.

Teaching Understanding and Supportive Behavior to Typically Developing Children

Social skills instruction in small groups for children with PDD is a start, but not enough. Performance and fluency of newly acquired social skills in all environments requires motivation and practice in those other environments. Children with PDD regularly establish a reputation as being odd or difficult. With that reputation comes expectations about how the child will behave. Sadly, these expectations often persist even after social learning and improvements have taken place. Thus, children with PDD are more likely than typically developing children to be rejected or ignored. Odd behaviors, including perseveration and preoccupations, failure to respond when spoken to, meltdowns, and inappropriate social behaviors make the child with PDD difficult to understand. Further, children with PDD who are over-initiators can come across as pushy and intrusive. While they are socially motivated, they are overly talkative and stick to their own agenda no matter what. Children with PDD who are under-initiators, by contrast, seem to just fade into the woodwork and may look like they do not want to play with others at all.

Children between the ages of 9 and 12 rated unfavorably a videotaped 12-year-old boy acting "autistic" whether they were told he had autism or not (Swaim & Morgan, 2001). Even mainstreamed preschool-age children behave differently toward their peers with disabilities than their nondisabled peers (Strain, 1984).

Typical children prefer to play with children at their own developmental level – they prefer typical peers. In general, typical peers, at best, are not sure of how to initiate an interaction or are afraid of the child with PDD. At worst, they shun or even bully the child with PDD. Poor response from peers can exacerbate a child's difficulties in establishing friendships and reduce motivation to try. Therefore, it is important to educate typical peers about individual differences as well as develop tolerance and a sense of fairness and promote initiations toward peers with PDD.

The child with PDD needs the opportunity to try her new social skills in an accepting and supportive environment. Without this type of school environment, social skills that develop in social skills training sessions will only be observed in those sessions. Fluency and generalization are encouraged by helping the children with PDD to practice their newly acquired social skills in all environments. This includes in the classroom and during lunch and recess every day.

As discussed below, the S.O.S. program develops understanding and supportive behavior in the typical peers of children with PDD through (a) peer education in the classroom for all children and (b) peer mentoring. These classroom lessons sensitize children to individual differences and encourage tolerance and fairness as well as social initiations towards their peers with differences. Further, peer mentoring supports the social behaviors of children with PDD during unstructured times of the school day.

Social Skills Lessons in the Classroom: Peer Education

The second major component of the S.O.S. program consists of classroom lessons geared toward developing an attitude of fairness and tolerance and an understanding that all people have strengths and weaknesses and deserve to be treated with respect. Teachers have a unique opportunity to foster a classroom community based on an understanding and acceptance of each other's strengths and weaknesses and a willingness to support each other in times of difficulty.

The major intent of the S.O.S. classroom lessons is to establish a peer-mediated approach to intervention in the classroom that promotes appropriate initiations toward children with PDD. When typical children play with typical peers, they tend to share, compliment each other, and suggest ideas for play. By comparison, when they play with peers with disabilities, they give physical help and engage in conflict management (Strain, 1984). It is important to teach typical children that they can also initiate and interact with their peers with PDD by sharing, complimenting, and suggesting ideas.

Peer education in the classroom is accomplished in the S.O.S. program through structured activities focused on classroom rules regarding fairness and tolerance, how it feels to be treated unfairly, the concept that all people have strengths and weaknesses, and being assertive rather than passive or aggressive in expressing feelings and ideas. One classroom lesson is given each week for the first five weeks of school, followed by bi-monthly booster lessons for the remainder of the school year.

An accepting classroom environment is a necessary component of any social skills program in school, as it helps typical children and children with PDD to initiate and respond appropriately to each other's initiations. But it is not sufficient for generalization of skills. Children with PDD need prompting in all environments before they are able to use a given social skill spontaneously across environments.

Peer Mentoring

The third major component of the S.O.S. program – peer mentoring – allows trained typical peers to provide prompts during the least structured and most difficult times of the school day for children with PDD – lunch and recess. Indeed, the most common behavior among children with PDD on the playground during recess is walking the periphery of the playground in isolation. In the S.O.S. program, same-age peers prompt and model appropriate social skills for the children with PDD in an effort to bring them into social interactions.

Direct prompting by peers has been found to produce immediate and significant increases in the responsiveness of the child with PDD as well as in the length of positive social interactions between typical peers and children with PDD (Shafer, Egel, & Neef, 1984). Mentors facilitate play interactions and coach the children with PDD to use the skills they are learning in their pull-out social skills sessions on the playground. The same-age mentors have the skills to engage the child with PDD, and who knows better than children what children play at their age? Most often adults who act as individual assistants to the child with PDD in the classroom cannot support social interaction during the less structured parts of the school day. Besides, their focus is usually on the child's safety ("Put on your coat." "Don't run with that other child. You'll fall!"). In addition, most children do not socialize in a typical manner with an adult watching.

Peer mentor training. Peer mentors are recruited during the classroom lessons, and parental permission is obtained before students start mentor training. In beginning a program like this, it is often difficult to recruit mentors. However, after the first year recruitment is easy as the children generally come to see the role as peer mentor as highly prestigious. Most children who end up mentoring are social leaders for all the right reasons, and other children begin to emulate them. Each child with PDD has three to four mentors, each responsible for supporting the child during lunch and recess one day a week. In reality, often all the peer mentors play together, including the child with PDD, all week.

The mentors receive five training lessons at the beginning of the school year, one per week (see page 207). These lessons focus on helping others; supporting strategies for emotional modulation; helping children with PDD to observe social situations and understand the main idea of what they see; games they typically play, and what they have to do to bring the child they mentor into their games; dealing with preoccupations; and contingency plans in case there is a problem.

After completing the training, the mentors attend supervision sessions once a week. Here they review the lessons that the children with PDD receive in their pull-out sessions and have an opportunity to discuss and receive guidance regarding their interactions with the child they mentor. Supervision sessions allow the mentors to monitor their interactions with the children with PDD, thereby promoting continued initiations toward those children.

The same adult who teaches the social skills pull-out lessons to the children being mentored provides training and supervision to the mentors. In our years of implementing the program, we have found this to be essential to success. The reason is simple: The teacher must know both the children being mentored and their mentors. She must hear the perceptions of both and provide advice and support based on that knowledge. For example, it is not unusual for the child being mentored to reject the mentor's play suggestions. In such an instance, the supervisor may explain, for example, that the child with PDD is obsessed with trains and recommend that the mentor bring in a train book and engage the child in his preoccupation at first. Or the adult may create a game about the special interests of the child with PDD, teach it to the mentor, and then encourage the mentor to play it with the mentee. At the same time the adult can teach the child with PDD the games that the mentor plays at recess, thereby reducing anxiety through familiarity, and encourage the child with PDD to try the mentor's game. The adult also observes the children on the playground intermittently throughout the year and may intervene to facilitate the relationship between the child with PDD and the typical peers, as necessary.

Generalization of skills is an issue for the peer mentors just as it is for the children with PDD. For example, typical children do not necessarily generalize their supportive behaviors to children with social skills issues who are not the specified target of intervention. This idea must be incorporated into the training.

Parent Involvement

Parents are partners in social skills intervention for their children with PDD. Therefore, parent involvement is another major component of the S.O.S. program. In particular, it is important that parents be educated about diagnosis, available services, and how to advocate for their children.

Parents must also be educated about typical social development, interpreting and responding to their child's behavior, social skills interventions, and how to follow through at home to aid generalization and fluency. Just as the peer mentor is aware of the S.O.S. social skill of the week so must the parents. Thus, they must learn (a) methods for reinforcing the social rules and strategies their children are taught, (b) behavior intervention strategies, and (c) how to foster peer interactions for their children.

In addition to reinforcing social behaviors in naturalistic settings, parents can help children with PDD find out how these behaviors function for them in life. In the S.O.S. program homework is provided for each social skills pull-out lesson so that the parent is aware of the goal to be reinforced all week and has at least one structured activity to do with the child to reinforce that activity. In addition, the child's social skills notebook is used to facilitate communication between the social skills teacher and the parents (see pages 58-59).

Parent training. Raising a child with PDD is quite different from raising a typically developing child, and many of the assumptions about typically developing children do not hold true for children with PDD. As part of the S.O.S. program, bi-monthly parent meetings provide a forum in which parents can ask questions and clarify their understanding of their child's behavior, learning style, and social goals. In addition, parents learn ways to help their children use the rules for emotional modulation, graphic organizers (Dunn & Sebastian, 2000) to aid organization of expression and understanding of social situations and language, and the rules for successful play dates. They are also taught behavior intervention strategies and how to set limits.

Parents must also learn to help their children to evaluate and take responsibility for their own behavior to the extent possible at any given point in development. Further, parents must learn to help their children form friendships and to build a social network. Most typically developing kids have stable best friendships by fourth grade (Frankel, 1996; McGuire & Weisz, 1982). Such close peer relationships are important because they are related to higher self-esteem, less anxiety and depression (Buhrmeister, 1990), and better ability to cope (Miller & Ingham, 1976). In addition, children learn through such relationships about trust and confiding in others, that friends can resolve conflicts, and so on.

Parents may need help in establishing social networks with other parents to set up play dates for their child. Through the parent meetings, teachers can encourage parents to form friendships with the parents of their child's peers to facilitate interaction with peers outside of school. As stated earlier, children with PDD do not learn social rules by watching their peers. They require direct instruction. Many parents will need support in providing direct instruction in how to play and interact reciprocally, including how to share, how to attend to and understand the other child's needs and feelings, how to converse, and how to resolve conflicts.

Parents must also be educated about current research on which social interventions are most likely to be effective and the way a child with PDD thinks. A common suggestion for developing social skills in children with PDD is to get them involved in structured activities like team sports. However, these are only a possible starting point for developing friendships and are not significantly related to social adjustment in and of themselves (Ladd & Price, 1987). It is the interaction before and after the games and structured activities that fosters closer relationships (Parke & Bhavnagri, 1989).

In sum, social skills taught in school, the environment in which the child with PDD spends most of his time with his peers, can be very effective. However, in order for new social skills to generalize, they must be reinforced through specific practice with teachers and peers in school, at home, and in other environments outside of school. A combined peer- and adult-mediated approach that includes parent education has the greatest likelihood of successfully teaching appropriate social behaviors as substitutes for inappropriate ones. The neuropsychological profile of the majority of children with PDD indicates that at least initially an approach in which the child is directly taught social rules and strategies for both behavioral modulation and processing information is optimal. The S.O.S. program was developed with all of these issues in mind.

Before we turn to the S.O.S. curriculum itself, we will review what it takes to implement the program successfully in terms of materials, staff time and commitment, as well as special instructional accommodations.

NOTE:

While it is possible for professionals in the field of autism to implement individual lessons from the S.O.S. program without the benefit of supervision, implementation of the complete program is a logistical challenge, and requires supervision by someone who is trained and well versed in the S.O.S. program. For school staff who deliver the lessons, supervision is essential to interpreting the responses of children to the program and to individualizing the work.

To promote successful implementation of the program, it is recommended that each school district implementing the program have a trained S.O.S. supervisor. School staff members with expertise and experience working with verbal children with autism spectrum disorders, who are interested in being trained as district supervisors, should contact the author at mdunn54@nyc.rr.com for the schedule and location of training sessions.

IMPLEMENTATION
OF THE S.O.S. PROGRAM

Materials

In addition to the S.O.S. manual, various kinds of materials are required to implement the social skills program. Most are part of a typical classroom.

- loose-leaf paper
- butcher block paper
- index cards
- shoebox
- markers
- pencils
- chalk*
- blackboard*
- 2 containers
- paper stoplights
- tape recorder
- music tapes
- mirror
- building blocks
- deck of cards
- board games
- balls for kickball, basketball and catch
- jump rope

*A dry-erase board or similar writing surface with appropriate writing tools may be substituted

Books

The following books should also be available for use in the lessons, where indicated:

Blubber, Judy Bloom (New York: Bantam Doubleday Dell Publishing Group, 1974)

The Brand New Kid, Katherine Couric (New York: Doubleday and Company, 2000)

Chrysanthemum, Kevin Henkes (New York: Green Willow Books, 1991)

"The Dream," In *Frog and Toad Together,* Arnold Lobel (New York: Harper Collins Children's Books, 1979)

The Giving Tree, Shel Silverstein (New York: Harper Collins Publishers, 1964)

Let's Talk About Feeling Angry, Joy Berry (Scholastic Inc., 1995)

Norma Jean Jumping Bean, Joanna Cole, illustrated by Lynn Munsinger (New York: Random House Children's Books, 2003)

Random Acts of Kindness, Rosalynn Carter (Berkeley, CA: Conari Press, 1994)

The Elephant's Pillow, Diana Reynolds Roome (Farrar, Straus and Giroux, 2003)

School Staff Commitment to Implement the Program

The following is an overview of typical school staff involved in implementation of the S.O.S. program and their respective roles.

The **social skills trainer/peer mentor supervisor** delivers social skills pull-out lessons to children with PDD and selects, trains, and supervises the peer mentors. This staff member also delivers the classroom lessons in collaboration with the classroom teachers in the classes that contain the children with PDD. The social trainer/peer mentor supervisor may be a speech/language pathologist, guidance counselor, resource room teacher, self-contained classroom teacher, or a psychologist who has knowledge of and experience working with children with PDD.

Classroom teachers who have children with PDD in their classes deliver classroom lessons with the aid of the social skills trainer/peer mentor supervisor.

The **S.O.S. program supervisor** is an expert in PDD and, ideally, certified in the S.O.S. program. While it is possible for professionals in the field of autism to implement individual lessons from the S.O.S. program without the benefit of supervision, implementation of the complete program is a logistical challenge, and requires supervision by someone who is well versed in the program (see page 22 for information concerning S.O.S. school supervisor certification).

To start implementation of the program, school staff (including general education teachers, speech language pathologists, guidance counselors, resource room teachers, self-contained classroom teachers, school psychologists and any other staff that wants the training), as well as parents of children with PDD, receive training in PDD and the S.O.S. social skills intervention from a PDD expert knowledgeable about the S.O.S. program. The training typically occurs as a two-day workshop.

From that time on, school staff carry out the program. Supervision sessions are held once a month for two hours. It is important that the S.O.S. supervisor observe the children in the program on a regular basis to provide appropriate recommendations. Supervision is essential to organizing and establishing the program, to interpreting the motives and behavior of the children with PDD, and to learning to individualize the program. By the end of the first year of implementation, selected speech/language pathologists, guidance counselors, resource room teachers, school psychologists, and self-contained classroom teachers are trained as social skills trainers. In our experience it takes two academic years to get the program fully up and running and the school staff to be comfortable implementing it.

The S.O.S. program supervisor may be an autism consultant hired by the school who is already S.O.S. certified. At the end of two academic years, one school staff member who is a certified S.O.S. therapist can be selected as the in-school supervisor, who continues monitoring and supervising the program after the autism consultant finishes training the staff and leaves the school. This has been the model for successful implementation of the program thus far.

An alternative is to send a staff member to be trained and certified as an S.O.S. program supervisor by the author of this curriculum and her staff. In addition to training in the components of the program and the logistics of getting the program going, one academic year of supervised implementation of the S.O.S. program and certification as an S.O.S. therapist is required for certification as an S.O.S. supervisor.

Timeline

- **Prior to Start of School Year:** A two-day training workshop taught by the S.O.S. program supervisor is held for social skills trainers/mentor supervisors and classroom teachers. In this workshop the staff receives training in the PDD spectrum, including diagnostic criteria, cognition, language, motor and sensory issues, socialization issues, aberrant behaviors, and emotional modulation. Videotapes are often used to show examples. A clear rationale for the structure of the program is also presented. Staff is oriented to the organization of the program and each component of the curriculum, and instruction is given in the use of graphic organizers to improve organization of expression, conversational skills, higher-order language comprehension, and perception of social situations. Demonstrations of specific lessons are provided and the staff has an opportunity to try key lessons, particularly those having to do with conversational skills.

As detailed later, separate training and meetings are held for parents of both children with PDD and mentors.

- **First Two Weeks of School:** Social skills trainers/mentor supervisors meet with teachers, lunchroom, and recess supervisors to discuss the program and its implementation.

- **Second Week of School:** Classroom lessons begin.

- **Second Week of School:** Pull-out lessons start.

- **Last Week of September:** Peer mentors are recruited. Their sessions, beginning with training, start the first week of October.

- **Second Week of November:** A pizza party or similar social event is held to introduce children with PDD to their mentors after mentor training is complete. Mentors begin interacting with the children with PDD during lunch and recess (at their weekly scheduled time) immediately following the party.

- **End of November:** Mentors are observed by the social skills trainers/mentor supervisors on the playground as they interact with children with PDD. They receive feedback during their supervision sessions.

Time Required to Deliver Lessons and Supervise Staff

- Social skills trainers/mentor supervisors meet with the S.O.S. program supervisor for two hours per month. Classroom teachers, parents, and social skills trainers/mentor supervisors stay in touch via e-mail and phone as needed with the S.O.S. supervisor between supervision sessions.

- The S.O.S. program supervisor holds one parent meeting every two months. Parent contact between meetings takes place via e-mail, phone, and the social skills notebook that each child brings back and forth between home and school (see pages 58-59).

- The social skills trainer/mentor supervisor has the following commitment for *each* social skills group:

  - One hour per week pull-out session for children with PDD in intervention

  - 30-45 minutes per week mentor training and supervision

  - One session per week for the first five weeks of school social skills lessons in the general education classrooms. Four booster classroom lessons bi-monthly throughout the rest of the academic year

  - Approximately 30-45 minutes per week preparation time to photocopy handouts and set up materials for the sessions

Successful Delivery of the S.O.S. Curriculum

Successful implementation of the S.O.S. program not only involves providing the pull-out lessons, classroom lessons, peer mentor training, and parent education, it also involves tailoring the program to individual children and requires a particular style of teaching the children.

Individualizing the curriculum for each child. The curriculum may be individualized to accommodate over-initiators versus under-initiators, issues with emotional regulation, avoidant behavior, controlling behavior, flexibility, and perseverative behaviors. This is accomplished by developing and assigning personal goals to each child. The social skills trainer decides the personal goal based on information obtained from the parents, feedback from the classroom teacher, and his or her own observations. At the beginning of the school year, parents and teachers are asked to provide a written list of their top-three major behavioral/social concerns about the child to the social skills trainer. Throughout the year, progress in these areas and new or continuing concerns are discussed at team meetings. An example of a personal goal for a child who under-initiates is: "I will raise my hand in class and ask one question each day." A personal goal for a child who talks obsessively on his own topic might be, "Ask another person what he would like to talk about and listen to what he says."

Special considerations for non-readers. To support non-readers or early readers in using the S.O.S. program, pictures (drawings or photos) should accompany all written information. A computer program like Kidspiration® (Helfgott & Westhaver, 2004) may be used to generate graphic organizers containing pictures. In addition, instead of asking the children to copy the social rules off the board, handouts may be made containing the rules, again accompanied by pictures. The children put these handouts into their social skills notebooks so that their parents and teachers can look at the rules and reinforce them, thereby helping the children to memorize them. Social rules may also be tape recorded.

VISUAL SUPPORTS
RULES: HOW DO I STOP?

• Take a deep breath   • Count to 10 slowly   • Say to myself, "I can stop"

Effective teaching style. As stated throughout this chapter, direct teaching is the recommended approach. Every lesson must emphasize the need for the child to stop prior to acting and the fact that the new rules are alternatives to old inappropriate behaviors. Each child should be prompted at the level necessary to ensure his or her attention. For some children, a physical prompt (a hand on the child's back) is better than a visual prompt, and a visual prompt is always stronger than a purely auditory prompt. Each child should be taught to seek prompts when needed, specifically to request help or modeling when confused about what to do.

Predictability is very important; indeed, it is sometimes essential to success for children with PDD. Predictability improves attention, reduces anxiety and perseveration, and eases transitions. Lack of predictability, by contrast, increases anxiety and inappropriate behaviors. Therefore, to increase success, each situation the child will encounter should be made as predictable as possible. This may be accomplished through visual schedules and cue cards carried by the child to aid transitions; for example, by helping him to remember how to behave exiting and entering classrooms and walking through the halls, as illustrated below.

CUE CARDS

1. I can only leave the classroom when the teacher says it's O.K.

2. I must walk, not run, in the hall.

Expectations and limits must be clear. They should be articulated and written down. Rewards and consequences likewise should be clear. It also is essential to support parents in setting limits for their children. High expectations in a supportive environment develop a sense of responsibility and independence in children. Like all parents, parents of children with PDD use varying approaches to child rearing. Likewise, teachers use varying approaches to teaching. Some respond to the child's issues with emotional modulation (meltdowns), and to weaknesses in socialization by avoiding situations that elicit strong emotions. They may expect that the child should not have to comply with rules that apply to others their age, even when their child is cognitively highly capable.

It is important for parents and teachers alike to set limits and make demands at a level at which the child can succeed. Strong emotions and difficult situations should not be avoided. Similarly, children should not be allowed to do whatever they want just to avoid upsetting them. Rather, children should be taught strategies for coping through direct instruction with high expectations in a supportive, loving environment. Success in meeting current demands and complying with limits increases motivation and compliance, which are essential for success in meeting future demands in school and in life beyond school.

The remainder of this book consists of the following:
- classroom curriculum, including booster sessions
- social skills pull-out lessons
- peer mentoring lessons
- parent training materials

S.O.S. References

Attwood, T. (2003). *Why does Chris do that? Some suggestions regarding the cause and management of the unusual behavior of children and adults with autism and Asperger Syndrome* (rev. ed.). Shawnee Mission, KS: Autism Asperger Publishing Company.

Baker, J. (2003). *Social skills training for children and adolescents with Asperger Syndrome and social-communication problems.* Shawnee Mission, KS: Autism Asperger Publishing Company.

Bauminger, N., & Kasari, C. (2000). Loneliness and friendships in high-functioning children with autism. *Child Development, 71,* 447-456.

Belchic, J. K., & Harris, S. L. (1994). The use of multiple peer examplars to enhance the generalization of play skills to the siblings of children with autism. *Child and Family Behavior Therapy, 16*(2), 1-25.

Bieber, J. (Producer). (1994). *Learning disabilities and social skills with Richard Lavoie: Last one picked … First one picked on.* Washington, DC: Public Broadcasting Service.

Buggey, T. (1999). Videotaped self-modeling: Allowing children to be their own models. *Teaching Exceptional Children, 4,* 27-31.

Buhrmeister, D. (1990). Intimacy of friendship, interpersonal competence, and adjustment during preadolescence and adolescence. *Child Development, 61,* 101-111.

Burack, J. A., Root, R., & Zigler, E. (1997). Inclusive education for students with autism: Reviewing ideological, empirical, and community considerations. In D. J. Cohen & F. Volkmar (Eds.), *Handbook of autism and pervasive developmental disorders* (pp. 796-807). New York: Wiley.

Capps L., Sigman M., & Yirmiya, N. (1995). Self-competence and emotional understanding in high-functioning children with autism. *Developmental & Psychopathology, 7,* 137-149.

Cardon, T. (2004). *Let's talk emotions: Helping children with social cognitive deficits, including AS, HFA, and NVLD, learn to understand and express empathy and emotions.* Shawnee Mission, KS: Autism Asperger Publishing Company.

Charlop-Christy, M. H., & Daneshvar, S. (2003). Using video modeling to teach perspective taking to children with autism. *Journal of Positive Behavior Interventions, 5,* 12-21.

Charlop-Christy, M. H., Le, L., & Freeman, K. A. (2000). A comparison of video modeling with in-vivo modeling for teaching children with autism. *Journal of Autism and Developmental Disorders, 30,* 537-552.

Charlop, M. H., & Milstein, J. P. (1989). Teaching autistic children conversational speech using video modeling. *Journal of Applied Behavior Analysis, 22,* 275-285.

Dowrick, P. W. (1999). A review of self modeling and related interventions. *Applied & Preventive Psychology, 8,* 23-39.

Duke, M. P., Nowicki, S., & Martin, E. A. (1996). *Teaching your child the language of social success.* Atlanta, GA: Peachtree.

Dunn, M. (in preparation). *Efficacy of a combined therapist- and peer-mediated social skills intervention for children with PDD in public schools.*

Dunn, M., & Sebastian, M. J. (2000). A neuropsychological approach to language intervention in autistic children. In P. J. Accardo, C. Magnusen, & A. J. Capute (Eds.), *Autism: Clinical and research issues* (pp. 57-75). Timonium, MD: York Press.

Frankel, F. (1996). *Good friends are hard to find: Help your child find, make, and keep friends.* Los Angeles: Perspective Publishing.

Gajewski, N., Hirn P., & Mayo, P. (1993). *Social star: General interaction skills (Book 1).* Eau Claire, WI: Thinking Publications.

Gajewski, N., Hirn, P., & Mayo, P. (1994). *Social star: Peer interaction skills (Book 2).* Eau Claire, WI: Thinking Publications.

Garcia-Winner, M. (2003). *Thinking about you, thinking about me: Philosophy and strategies for facilitating the development of perspective taking for students with social cognitive deficits.* London: Jessica Kingsley Publishers.

Gray, C. (1994a). *Comic strip conversations.* Arlington, TX: Future Horizons.

Gray, C. (1994b). *The new social story book.* Arlington, TX: Future Horizons.

Gresham, F. M., Sugai, G., & Horner, R. H. (2001). Interpreting outcomes of social skills training for students with high-incidence disabilities. *Exceptional Children, 67,* 331-344.

Gutstein, S. E., & Sheely, R. K. (2002). *Relationship development intervention with young children: Social and emotional development activities for Asperger Syndrome, autism, PDD and NLD.* London: Jessica Kingsley Publishers.

Haring, T., & Breen, C. (1992). A peer mediated social network intervention to enhance the social integration of persons with moderate and severe disabilities. *Journal of Applied Behavior Analysis, 25,* 319-333.

Helfgott, D., & Westhaver, M. (2004). *Kidspiration® Software.* Vancouver WA: Inspiration Software®, Inc.

Howlin, P., Baron-Cohen, S., & Hadwin, J. (1999). *Teaching children with autism to mind-read: A practical guide.* New York: John Wiley & Sons.

Kamps, D. M., Barbetta, P. M., Leonard, B. R., & Delquadri, J. (1994). Classwide peer tutoring: An integration strategy to improve reading skills and promote peer interactions among students with autism and general education peers. *Journal of Applied Behavior Analysis, 27*(1), 49-61.

Kamps, D. M., Leonard, B. R., Vernon, S., Dugan, E. P., Delquadri, J. C., Gershon, B., Wade, L., & Folk, L. (1992). Teaching social skills to students with autism to increase peer interactions in an integrated first-grade classroom. Journal of *Applied Behavior Analysis, 25*(2), 281-288.

Kamps, D. M., Potucek, J., Lopez, A., Kravits, T., & Kemmerer, K. (1997). The use of peer networks across multiple settings to improve social interaction for students with autism. *Journal of Behavioral Education, 7,* 335-357.

Kasari, C., Freeman, S., Bauminger, N., & Alkin, M. (1999). Parental perceptions of inclusion: Effects of autism and Down syndrome. *Journal of Autism and Developmental Disorders, 29,* 297-305.

Koegel, L. K., Koegel, R. L., Frea, W. D., & Fredeen, R. M. (2001). Identifying early intervention targets for children with autism in inclusive school settings. *Behavior Modification, 25*(5), 745-761.

Ladd, G. W., & Price, J. M. (1987). Predicting children's social and school adjustment following the transition from preschool to kindergarten. *Child Development, 58,* 1168-1189.

Lewis, B. (1998). *What do you stand for?* Minneapolis, MN: Free Spirit Publishing.

Lord, C., & Hopkins, J. M. (1986). The social behavior of autistic children with younger and same-age nonhandicapped peers. *Journal of Autism and Developmental Disorders, 16*(3), 249-262.

Lord, C., Risi, S., Lambrecht, L., Cook, E. H., Leventhal, B. L., DiLavore, P. C., Pickles, A., & Rutter, M. (2000). The Autism Diagnostic Observation Schedule–Generic: A standard measure of social and communication deficits associated with the spectrum of autism. *Journal of Autism and Developmental Disorders, 30,* 205-223.

Marriage, K. J., Gordon, V., & Brand, L. (1995). A social skills group for boys with Asperger's syndrome. *Australian and New Zealand Journal of Psychiatry, 29,* 58-62.

Matson, J. L., & Swiezy, N. (1994). Social skills training with autistic children. In L. Mason (Ed.), *Autism in children and adults: Etiology, assessment and intervention* (pp. 24-26). Pacific Grove, CA: Brooks Cole.

McAfee, J. (2001). *Navigating the social world: A curriculum for individuals with Asperger's Syndrome, high functioning autism and related disorders.* Arlington, TX: Future Horizons.

McClannahan, L. E., & Krantz, P. J. (1999). *Activity schedules for children with autism: Teaching independent behavior.* Bethesda, MD: Woodbine House.

McConnell, S. R. (2002). Interventions to facilitate social interaction for young children with autism: Review of available research and recommendations for educational intervention and future research. *Journal of Autism and Developmental Disorders, 32,* 351-372.

McGinnis, E., & Goldstein, A. P. (1997). *Skillstreaming the elementary school child.* Champaign, IL: Research Press.

McGuire, K. D., & Weisz, J. R. (1982). Social cognition and behavior correlates of preadolescent chumship. *Child Development, 53,* 1478-1484.

Mesibov, G. B. (1984). Social skills training with verbal autistic adolescents and adults: A program model. *Journal of Autism and Other Developmental Disabilities, 14,* 395-404.

Miller, P. M., & Ingham, J. G. (1976). Friends, confidants, and symptoms. *Social Psychiatry, 11,* 51-58.

Minshew, N. J., Goldstein, G., & Siegel, D. J. (1997). Neuropsychologic functioning in autism: Profile of a complex information processing disorder. *Journal of International Neuropsychological Society, 3*(4), 303-316.

Moyes, R. A., & Moreno, S. J. (2001). *Incorporating social goals in the classroom: A guide for teachers and parents of children with high-functioning autism and Asperger Syndrome.* Philadelphia, PA: Taylor and Francis Group.

Myles, B., & Southwick, J. (2005). *Asperger Syndrome and difficult moments: Practical solutions for tantrums, rage and meltdowns. New Revised and Expanded Edition.* Shawnee Mission, KS: Autism Asperger Publishing Company.

Odom, S. L., & Strain, P. S. (1984). Peer-mediated approaches to promoting children's social interaction: A review. *American Journal of Orthopsychiatry, 54,* 544-557.

Odom, S. L., & Watts, E. (1991). Reducing teacher prompts in peer-mediated interventions for young children with autism. *Journal of Special Education, 25,* 26-43.

Ozonoff, S., & Miller, J. N. (1995). Teaching theory of mind: A new approach to social skills training for individuals with autism. *Journal of Autism and Developmental Disorders, 25,* 415-433.

Parke, R. D., & Bhavnagri, N. P. (1989). Parents as managers of children's peer friendships. In D. Belle (Ed.), *Children's social networks and social supports* (pp. 241-259). New York: Wiley.

Pierce, K., & Schreibman, L. (1997). Multiple peer use of pivotal response training to increase social behaviors of classmates with autism: Results from trained and untrained peers. *Journal of Applied Behavior Analysis, 30,* 157-160.

Rogers, S. J. (2000). Interventions that facilitate socialization in children with autism. *Journal of Autism and Developmental Disorders, 30,* 399-409.

Rumsey, J. M., & Hamburger, S. D. (1988). Neuropsychological findings in high-functioning men with infantile autism, residual state. *Journal of Clinical and Experimental Neuropsychology, 10*(2), 201-210.

Sainato, D. M., Goldstein, H., & Strain, P. S. (1992). Effects of self-evaluation on preschool children's use of social interaction strategies with their classmates with autism. *Journal of Applied Behavior Analysis, 25,* 127-141.

Schopler, E., & Mesibov, G. B. (Eds.). (1983). *Autism in adolescents and adults.* New York: Plenum Press.

Shafer, M. S., Egel, A. L., & Neef, N. A. (1984). Training mildly handicapped peers to facilitate changes in the social interaction skills of autistic children. *Journal of Applied Behavior Analysis, 17*(4), 461-476.

Stainback, W., & Stainback, S. (1984). A rationale for the merger of special and regular education. *Exceptional Children, 51*(2), 102-111.

Strain, P. (1984). Social behavior patterns of nonhandicapped and developmentally disabled friend pairs in mainstream preschools. *Analysis & Intervention in Developmental Disabilities, 4,* 1.

Swaim, K. F., & Morgan, S. B. (2001). Children's attitudes and behavioral intentions toward a peer with autistic behaviors: Does a brief educational intervention have an effect? *Journal of Autism and Developmental Disorders, 31*(2), 195-205.

Twemlow, S. W., Fonagy, P., Sacco, F. C., Gies, M. L., Evans, R., & Ewbank, R. (2001). Creating a peaceful school learning environment: A controlled study of an elementary school intervention to reduce violence. *American Journal of Psychiatry, 158,* 808-810.

Villa, R., & Thousand, J. (1995). *Creating an inclusive school.* Alexandria, VA: Association for Supervision and Curriculum Development.

Volden J., & Johnston, J. (1999). Cognitive scripts in autistic children and adolescents. *Journal of Autism and Developmental Disorders, 29,* 203-211.

Volkmar, F. R., & Klin, A. (1998). Asperger syndrome and nonverbal learning disabilities. In E. Schopler, G. B. Mesibov, & L. J. Kunce (Eds.), *Asperger syndrome or high functioning autism?* (pp. 107-121). New York: Plenum Press

Wolfberg, P. J., & Schuler, A. L. (1993). Integrated play groups: A model for promoting the social and cognitive dimensions of play in children with autism. *Journal of Autism and Developmental Disorders, 23,* 467-489.

S.O.S. Classroom Curriculum

Overview

The S.O.S. classroom curriculum is taught in the general education classroom to help develop an accepting environment for children with social skills needs.

Goals

The goals of the classroom curriculum are to strengthen:

- A sense of community
- A sense of fairness
- A sense of self and others (through an understanding of every child's strengths and weaknesses)

Staff and Time Commitment

1. One lesson per week during weeks 2-6 of the school year
2. Four booster lessons in November, January, March, May

Note: Classroom teachers and S.O.S. pull-out staff can teach lessons together.

Lessons Timeline

Classroom lessons are taught in the general education classes for all children beginning the second week of school. Once the first five lessons have been completed, booster lessons follow bi-monthly.

Lesson #1 – Asking for and Offering Help

Lesson #2 – Class Rules About Behavior

Lesson #3 – Caring

Lesson #4 – Telling Others About Myself: Graphic Organizer About Self

Lesson #5 – Learning About Differences:

- How do I feel when someone acts or looks different from me?
- How does it feel to be different?

Booster Lessons

November-Booster Lesson #1: Understanding the Impact of Unkind Behaviors

January-Booster Lesson #2: Demonstrating Kindness to Others

March-Booster Lesson #3: Having the Courage to Make a Difference in Someone's Life

May-Booster Lesson #4: Being Assertive When Rights Are Violated

Materials

For a listing of general materials used throughout the curriculum, see page 24.

Lesson #1: ASKING FOR AND OFFERING HELP

GOAL:

This is an open discussion of helping and why it is important to help others and offer help.

1. Talk about the concept of community and point out that not everyone is good at everything, but that when we join together as a group we can do more than any one of us could do alone. Point out that everyone has strengths and weaknesses and that we must support each other. All students, including those with special needs, take part in this discussion.

2. Discuss classroom rules about helping and have the children write them out. Children might volunteer to make posters of the rules to be put up in the classroom.

RULES FOR ASKING FOR HELP	RULES FOR GIVING HELP
• Interrupt appropriately. • Clearly say what you need help with. • Listen. • If you do not understand, patiently ask questions. • Say thank you.	• You may give help if you are asked. • Ask "Can I help you?," but *only* give help if the person says *yes*. • Listen. • If you do not understand, patiently ask questions. • Help if you can or find someone who can help.

3. Introduce the concept of peer mentors. Discuss who they are and what they do. Explain that the peer mentors are trained and supervised same-age peers who support the social interactions of the children with weaknesses in social skills during lunch and recess (see also pages 19-20). *Note:* For the sake of confidentiality, do NOT discuss diagnosis. Also, do not discuss individual children.

   • Write the two jobs of peer mentors on the board:

     – to help children from their class to join in at lunch and on the playground

     – to help resolve conflicts

   • Talk about how special the job of peer mentor is and announce that students may volunteer for the job.

4. Discuss peer mentoring over the next couple of days. Ask for volunteers and send letters home to parents (see page 210). Optimally, try to identify three to four mentors for each child with PDD in the program.

Classroom Curriculum

Lesson #2: CLASS RULES ABOUT BEHAVIOR

GOAL:

The focus of this lesson is on classroom rules for appropriate behavior, especially fairness, and on creating an understanding of how people feel when they are treated unfairly. The idea is to encourage the children to treat each other fairly and teach them how. However, it is also important that children recognize that unfair situations do occur from time to time and that they must know how to appropriately deal with feeling unfairly treated.

1. Start by playing the "How Does It Feel to Be Treated Unfairly" relay outlined below. DO NOT tell the children the name of the game or the purpose.

"How Does It Feel to Be Treated Unfairly" Relay

- Divide the class into two teams. (The teams do not need to consist of even numbers of children.)

- Have two teams stand behind two starting lines.

- Mark two lines several yards away.

- When you say "go," one child at a time runs across the room, touches the line on the floor, and comes back. Then the next child in the line does the same, and so on.

Note: This runs like a regular relay, with the winners being the team whose last runner crosses the finish line first. However, the catch is that you keep changing the rules, giving the teams an unfair advantage at different points in the game.

For example, you may ask all the children to take off their shoes before running and put them back on after running (tied, buckled, etc.) before the next child on their team can run. After a couple of kids on each team have run, stop the game and say that one team's shoes are harder to get off and on. Therefore, that team may run to the line but the other team has to walk. Let a couple of more children run and stop the game again. This time say that the team you gave the advantage to does not have to put their shoes back on at all. Finally, stop them again; and tell them all to run, but the team that had the disadvantage does not have to take off their shoes at all.

They should all be complaining about unfairness at this point. Have them all sit down.

From *What Do You Stand For?* by Barbara A. Lewis. Minneapolis, MN: Free Spirit Publishing, 1998, pp.149-150. Used with permission.

Alternative

If you want a quieter game, have the children play a board game like *Monopoly.* You as the banker give different children different amounts of money to start, give properties to individual children for no reason throughout the game, let them pass "go" even if they are nowhere near it, etc. The point is to make the game feel very unfair to all involved.

Now, ask:

How did it feel to play the game?

How did it feel to be on the team or be the child that got the special chances to win?

How did it feel to be on the other team?

Does it matter if people are fair to others? Why or why not?

2. Write out the "Care & Be Fair" rules on the board and talk about each rule (define it).

RULES FOR CARE & BE FAIR

1. Treat others with respect.

2. Wait your turn.

3. Share.

4. Sit quietly so you do not disturb others.

5. Pay attention.

6. Listen to directions.

7. Remember your manners.

8. Do not engage in gossip or rumors.

9. Don't leave people out.

10. Never hit or grab from others.

---

3. Have the students read the "Care & Be Fair" rules. Choose 10 students and ask each of them to read a rule on the list, followed by the entire class saying, "Care & Be Fair." Ask: What is the most important rule?

   Answer: "Care & Be Fair."

4. Ask a student to volunteer to make a poster listing the 10 rules.

Lesson #3: Caring

GOAL:

This lesson is designed to reinforce the concept of caring and to expand on the concept of empathy.

1. Read *The Giving Tree* by Shel Silverstein (New York: Harper Collins Publishers, 1964) to the class.

2. Talk about empathy (knowing another person's feelings). Discuss the idea that not only is it important to say nice things to others, it is also important to try to understand how another person is feeling.

3. Discuss put-downs and put-ups. "Put-downs" are comments that are critical and hurtful. "Put-ups" are the opposite. They are compliments meant to encourage others. Make a list on the board of nice things the children can say to each other. Encourage them to give each other a "pat on the back" (put-up) on a regular basis.

4. For older children you may want to read aloud or assign a book like *Blubber* by Judy Bloom (New York: Bantam Doubleday Dell Publishing Group, 1974) to really bring the point home.

Lesson #4:
Telling Others About Myself:
GRAPHIC ORGANIZER ABOUT SELF

GOAL:

The purpose of this lesson is to discuss the fact that people are different in some ways and the same in others, and that everyone has strengths and weaknesses.

In this lesson children generate graphic organizers as a way to describe themselves to the class. A graphic organizer is a concrete, visual outline of a concept or description. Page 42 shows a sample graphic organizer called a description organizer.

The main topic to be described is written in the oval in the center. In this case the main topic is the child. Subtopics are listed in the ovals that surround the main topic. In this activity subtopics should include the children's likes (favorite TV show, movie, teacher, subject, etc.), dislikes, what children are good at/talents, and what they have trouble with. Hobbies, recent family trips, and family may also be included, or anything else the child would like the class to know. Photocopy the empty graphic organizer on page 42 and have the children fill it in. Children may work on this activity with their parents. With young children who are not yet reading, use pictures along with words. Examples of completed graphic organizers can be found on pages 43 and 44.

The children can either write the description and read it to the class or just use their graphic organizers to orally present themselves to the class. After each child's presentation, ask the class to comment on which strengths they have observed in the child who just presented. You might ask if any of the children are willing to demonstrate talents in class (e.g., dancing, singing, juggling).

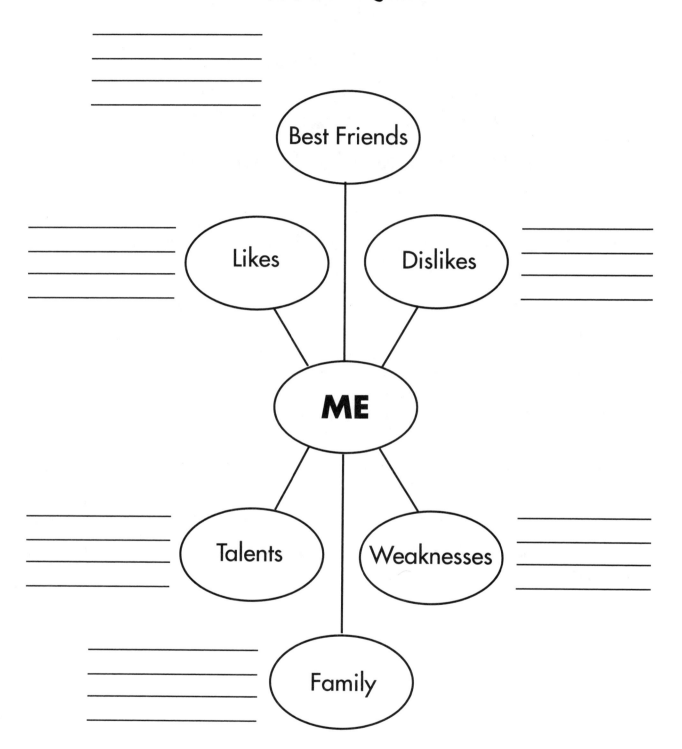

Sample Description Organizer #1

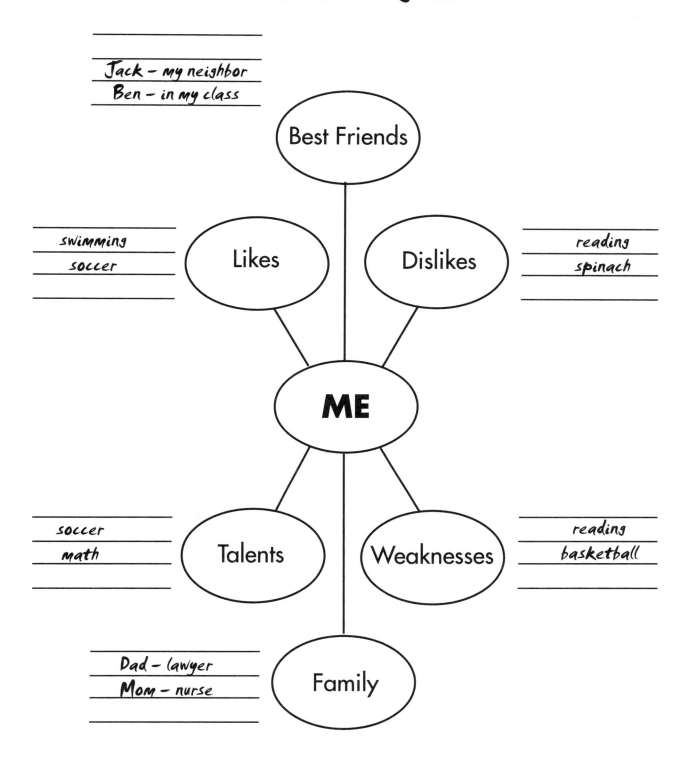

Jack – my neighbor
Ben – in my class

Best Friends

swimming
soccer

Likes

reading
spinach

Dislikes

ME

soccer
math

Talents

reading
basketball

Weaknesses

Dad – lawyer
Mom – nurse

Family

Sample Description Organizer #2
Using Visuals

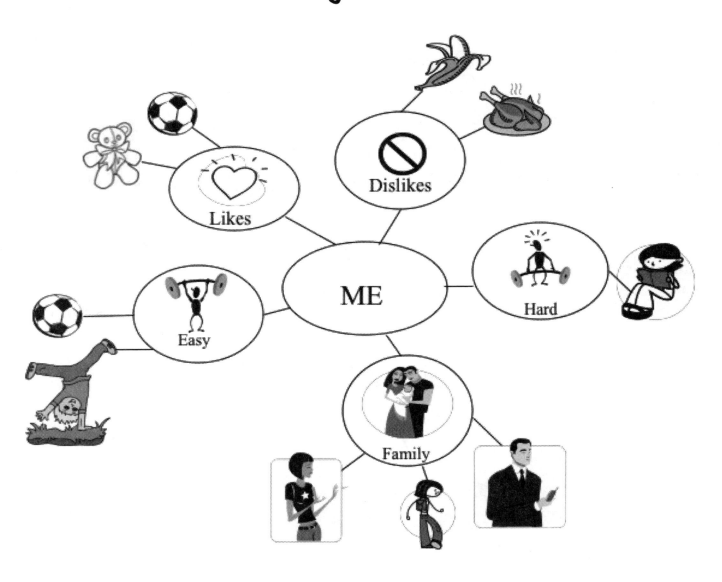

This graphic organizer was created with Kidspiration® (© 2004) Inspiration Software, Inc.

Lesson #5: Learning About Differences:

HOW DO I FEEL WHEN SOMEONE ACTS OR LOOKS DIFFERENT FROM ME? HOW DOES IT FEEL TO BE DIFFERENT?

GOAL:

The point of this lesson is to help children explore the questions: How do I feel when someone acts or looks different from me? and How does it feel to be different? through reading and discussing any of the following books. A variety of books deal with the subject of differences among people. Assign the readings to children individually and discuss in class or read the stories to the entire class. The books listed are merely suggestions. Any books on the topic are acceptable as long as the reading leads to exploration of the questions below in class.

After reading one of the following books (you may read to the class or ask the children to read), each child should answer the following questions in writing (younger children may get help from their parents):

- How is the main character in the book different from you?

- How did other children in the story treat that character?

- How do you feel when someone looks or acts differently from you?

- How does it feel to be different?

- How do you think you should treat children who are different from you?

A Very Special Friend (Grades K-3, Adult reads)
Author: Dorothy Hoffman Levi
Publisher: Gallaudet University Press, 1989
A lonely little girl named Frannie becomes friends with her new neighbor who happens to be deaf.

All About My Brother (Grades 1-3)
Author: Sarah Peralta
Publisher: Autism Asperger Publishing Company, 2002
An 8-year-old girl explains what it is like to have a nonverbal autistic brother.

Andy and His Yellow Frisbee (Grades K-3, Adult reads)
Author: Mary Thompson
Publisher: Woodbine House, 1996
Andy is a little boy who likes to play by himself and spin his yellow frisbee every day during recess. A new girl at school, Sarah, is curious about his behavior. Andy's older sister worries about what will happen when Sarah approaches Andy.

Blue Bottle Mystery: An Asperger Adventure (Grades 4-6)
Author: Kathy Hoopmann
Publisher: Jessica Kingsley Publishers, 2001
This story is a mystery about a blue bottle and a boy who is diagnosed with Asperger Syndrome. It emphasizes that knowing the boy's diagnosis helps others understand him.

Eukee: The Jumpy Jumpy Elephant (Grades K-3, Adult reads)
Authors: Clifford L. Corman and Esther Trevino
Publisher: Specialty Press, 1995
This is the story of Eukee, a little elephant with an attention deficit disorder. He is active and feels "jumpy." He goes to the doctor to get help.

Having a Brother Like David (Grades K-3, Adult reads)
Authors: Cindy Dolby Nollette and Others
Publisher: Minneapolis Children's Medical Center, 1985
This is a story about a boy who has a brother with autism. It points out how his brother looks like other kids but is different.

I'm Like You, You're Like Me: A Child's Book about Understanding and Celebrating Each Other (Grades 1-2)
Author: Cindy Gainer
Publisher: Free Spirit Publishing, Inc., 1998
This book discusses the ways that children are similar to each other but also different. It celebrates each child's uniqueness and shows children with differences working and playing together.

Oliver Onion (Grades K-4)
Author: Diane Murrell
Publisher: Autism Asperger Publishing Company, 2004
Oliver Onion is unhappy with himself and thinks that by changing his looks, he will lead a happier life. He soon learns to accept and capitalize on who he is.

See You Tomorrow, Charles (Grades K-3, Adult reads)
Author: Miriam Cohen
Publisher: Dell Publishing Company, 1997
This is a story about a blind boy named Charles and his first-grade class.

Someone Special, Just Like You (Grades 4-6)
Author: Tricia Brown
Publisher: Holt, Henry Books for Young Readers, 1995
This book focuses on the similarities between typically developing children and the peers with developmental disabilities. The main idea is that every child is special.

Booster Lesson #1 *
(November):
UNDERSTANDING THE IMPACT OF UNKIND BEHAVIORS

GOAL:

The purpose of this lesson is to facilitate thinking and discussion of ways in which people are influenced by the unkind behaviors of others.

1. Show the children the book *Chrysanthemum* by Kevin Henkes (New York: Green Willow Books, 1991) and give them a brief synopsis. Chrysanthemum is a little mouse who is just beginning school. The book tells the story of her first experience with the children at school and her feelings about how it goes.

2. Give each child a blank sheet of white paper and ask them to draw either a picture of Chrysanthemum the mouse or Chrysanthemum the flower (the flower does not have to look like a real chrysanthemum as pictured in the book; any drawing of a flower will do).

3. Read the book to the children. Each time Chrysanthemum's feelings are hurt, the children are to crumple their pictures. When something kind is said to Chrysanthemum, the children are to smooth out their drawings.

4. After reading the book, discuss the fact that even though nice things are later said to Chrysanthemum and she feels better, the paper, reflecting her feelings, is never perfectly smooth again. It continues to show the marks of the hurtful words spoken.

5. Review the concepts of "put-ups" and "put-downs."

(This lesson was adapted from a lesson by Martha Taylor, www.eduplace.com/tview/pages/c/Chrysanthemum_Kevin_Henkes.html).

*Booster lessons reinforce and extend what students learned about fairness and tolerance earlier in the school year.

Booster Lesson #2
(January):
DEMONSTRATING KINDNESS TO OTHERS

by Sheryl Chuzmir and Michelle Dunn

GOAL:

The purpose of this lesson is to facilitate thinking and discussion of ways in which people show each other kindness and the value of being kind.

1. For younger children read the book *The Elephant's Pillow* by Diana Reynolds Roome (Farrar, Strauss and Giroux, 2003) or another appropriate book about kind behaviors. For older children read some of the passages from the book *Random Acts of Kindness* by Rosalynn Carter (Berkeley, CA: Conari Press, 1994). Make a list on the board of acts of kindness mentioned in the book. Talk about the positive results of each act and the reasons why such acts are important.

2. Help children brainstorm specific examples of how they can show kindness to others at school and at home.

3. Give each child a sheet of lined loose-leaf paper. Have them fold it in half the long way to make two columns. Have them put the following headings at the top of each column: *Kindness at School* and *Kindness at Home* and add suggestions below each.

4. For younger children, give the students precut construction paper flower cut-outs, including petals, stems, and leaves. Ask the children to write 2-3 examples of acts of kindness on their flowers. Next, ask them to glue the flower petals, stems and leaves to a piece of construction paper. The flowers can be hung as a display or be compiled into a class book.

5. For older children, have them write their own paragraphs of acts of kindness (like those in *Random Acts of Kindness*) to be compiled and perhaps "published" in a class book.

Booster Lesson #3

(March):

HAVING THE COURAGE TO MAKE A DIFFERENCE IN SOMEONE'S LIFE

by Felice Silverman

GOAL:

The purpose of this lesson is to reinforce the concepts of kindness and compassion for others and to point out that at times showing compassion for others requires courage.

1. Read the book *The Brand New Kid* by Katherine Couric (New York: Doubleday and Company, 2000).

2. Discuss how the characters felt.

3. Discuss what Elle did and what qualities she has that make her a hero.

4. Write the following statement on the board, "Elle was the hero because_____."
    Have the children copy the statement onto the bottom of a large sheet of plain white paper and fill in the blank. Ask each child to draw a picture of what Elle did that made her a hero at the top of the paper.

5. Older children may be asked to write a paragraph including supporting details for why Elle was a hero.

Booster Lesson #4

(May):

BEING ASSERTIVE WHEN RIGHTS ARE VIOLATED

GOAL:

The purpose of this lesson is to discuss the concept of violation of a person's rights and the importance of being assertive rather than passive or aggressive when one's rights are violated.

1. Tell the students: "When something happens that upsets you, it is important to express your feelings appropriately. There are three ways people express such feelings. You can be *passive, aggressive,* or *assertive.*"

2. Discuss each term and brainstorm definitions for being *assertive, passive,* and *aggressive* with the class. Write the final definitions on the board.

   Sample Definitions:

   - <u>Being assertive:</u> *Standing up for your rights by telling your feelings and what you need without screaming, physically hurting, or cursing.*

   - <u>Being passive:</u> *Not standing up for yourself.*

   - <u>Being aggressive:</u> *Standing up for your rights with anger by physically hurting, screaming, yelling, or cursing.*

3. Read the appropriate version (depending on age; see the recommended ages for each story) of each of the following stories to the class. Tell the students that after the story is read, they will be asked to say whether the main character's behavior was passive, aggressive, or assertive.

Story 1
(recommended for grades 1-4)

Julia let her friend Victoria borrow her favorite toy. Victoria said she would give it back the next day. After four days Victoria still hadn't given Julia her toy back. When Julia asked Victoria for her toy back, Victoria said, "You're just going to have to wait because I want to play with it one more day." Julia said OK and walked away.

Was her behavior *passive, aggressive,* or *assertive?* Was her behavior appropriate? Should she have done anything differently?

(recommended for grades 5-7)

Jean loaned some money to Jack three days in a row so that he could buy lunch. He said he would pay her back the following Monday. After a couple of weeks Jack still hadn't paid Jean back. Jean asked Jack to repay the money as he had promised. Jack said, "You're just going to have to forget the money because I don't have any." Jean said OK and walked away.

Was her behavior *passive*, *aggressive*, or *assertive*? Was her behavior appropriate? Should she have done anything differently?

Story 2
(recommended for grades 1-4)

On the playground, Sheryl was waiting in line for a turn on a swing. She was next in line, but another kid went to get on the swing before her. At this point, Sheryl said, "Excuse me. I don't know if you saw me but I am the next person on line." The kid answered, "Sorry," and let Sheryl get on the swing next.

Was Sheryl's behavior *passive*, *aggressive*, or *assertive*? Was her behavior appropriate? Should she have done anything differently?

OR

(recommended for grades 5-7)

Susan was in the supermarket waiting in line to pay for some milk. She was the next customer in line, but the cashier kept waiting on all of the adults in line before her. Finally, Susan said, "Excuse me, miss. I don't know if you saw me, but I am the next person on line." The cashier immediately apologized and waited on Susan.

Was Susan's behavior *passive*, *aggressive*, or *assertive*? Was her behavior appropriate? Should she have done anything differently?

Story 3
(recommended for grades 1-4)

Jack's parents promised that they would take him to the toy store to buy a toy if his behavior was good at the doctor's office. Jack cooperated with the doctor. His parents said he did a good job, but added that there wouldn't be enough time to go to the toy store that day. Jack started to cry and yell at his parents.

Was his behavior *passive*, *aggressive*, or *assertive*? Was his behavior appropriate? Should he have done anything differently?

OR

(recommended for grades 5-7)

Miguel's parents promised him that he could go to the baseball game on Saturday with his best friend's family if he finished his social studies report before the weekend. He finished the report in time, but his parents had a change of plan and said that Miguel would not be able to go to the ballgame after all. Miguel looked at his parents and said, "I can't believe you won't let me go to that game!" He continued to yell at his parents for 10 minutes straight, then stormed out of the room.

Was his behavior *passive*, *aggressive*, or *assertive*? Was his behavior appropriate? Should he have done anything differently?

4. Discuss the idea that being assertive is the most appropriate way to behave when one's rights are violated. Explain that a person's rights are violated when a person is being taken advantage of, or is purposely hurt, teased, or ignored. Ask the children to provide examples of each type and write them on the board.

To elaborate and make sure the children understand, point out the following:

- Sometimes you will feel angry about something but when you stop and think about it, you don't really have a right to be angry. For example, if you do not hand in your science project until three days after the due date and your teacher drops your grade from what would have been a B+ to a C-, your rights have not been violated.

- You have a right to be angry if something is truly unfair but not if your rights have not been violated.

- If your rights or the rights of another person have been violated, you should express your feelings in an assertive way.

RULES FOR BEING ASSERTIVE

STOP

THINK: Is this person being unfair? Have your rights been violated?
      If no, you can tell someone else about how you feel, but it is wrong to argue for what you want (even in an assertive way).

GO: **If yes,** tell the person how you feel in a clear, firm way. Do not yell, threaten, or become physical.

THINK: Is the person responding in a fair way?

GO: If yes, say "thank you for listening to me."
     If no, or if the person does not respond or doesn't care, don't get stuck telling your feelings over and over again (that becomes aggressive). If you still need help dealing with someone who is unfair after you have tried all of this, talk to an adult.

---

5. Engage in role-play as suggested below.

- Demonstrate appropriate and inappropriate ways of expressing feelings and differences of opinion. The following situation is an example:

 You do yard work for the person who lives next-door. She has agreed to pay you every Friday. You have gone to her house to pick up your money. She didn't have money for you last week. You let it go because she said she didn't have time to get to the bank, but this week she doesn't have your pay either.

- Demonstrate each of three different reactions: *passive*, *aggressive*, and *assertive* and have the students decide whether the behavior was appropriate or inappropriate.

- Have kids role-play appropriate behavior in the following situations:

    - bullying (e.g., one child making fun of another child's clothes). The child role-playing the bullied person should demonstrate an assertive response. Add another child who can role-play an assertive response in support of the bullied child. Explain that if kids stick together and respond assertively to bullies, the bullying will stop.

    - appropriate and inappropriate touching (e.g., a child starts to play with another child's hair)

    - not waiting one's turn (e.g., a child cuts in line where a group of children are waiting to get on the swing or waiting to get a drink from the fountain)

6. Have the children break into groups to discuss the answers to the following questions (the group may select a secretary to write out the answers):

1. What is the very first thing you do before you decide to be assertive with someone?

2. What is wrong with being aggressive?

3. What is wrong with being passive?

4. Why is being assertive the best way to tell about your feelings when someone has been unfair or you have a difference of opinion?

5. What should you do if being assertive doesn't work with someone?

S.O.S.
Social Skills
Pull-Out
Lessons

Goals of S.O.S.
PULL-OUT LESSONS

In addition to participating in the S.O.S. curriculum delivered in the general education classroom, children on the PDD spectrum are seen for social skills pull-out lessons one hour per week to teach and rehearse social rules.

The goals of the S.O.S. pull-out lessons are to:

- develop the ability to modulate behavior and emotional responses
- learn social rules
- develop an understanding of main idea in language and social situations and responding in an organized way with a focus on the main idea
- reduce perseverations and preoccupations
- develop insight

Getting Started

1. The S.O.S. program is typically explained and recommended to the parents of high-functioning children with PDD by school staff. (This usually happens in the spring of the previous academic year.) If the parents consent to their child participating in the program, they are invited to a two-day training provided by the S.O.S. supervisor prior to the beginning of the school year (see page 225). If they cannot attend the scheduled training, school staff will hold a meeting to orient them to the program at another time.

2. Once parental permission has been obtained, ask parents to make sure their child brings a loose-leaf notebook with plenty of paper to each pull-out session. Divide the notebook into three sections: One section in the front is for social skills class work. The next section is for social skills homework, and the third section is for communication among and between staff and parents.

3. Obtain very specific input from each of the parents in the first month of school. Ask them to write the following in the communication section of the social skills notebook (see #2):
   - What are the five biggest problems your child currently encounters?
   - What are your child's strengths?
   - What are your greatest concerns and what do you see as the child's social skills needs? (If the parents have not discussed the answers to these questions with their child and feel that it is not appropriate to do so at this time, then instead of including them in the notebook, the answers to these questions may be sent under separate cover.)

4. Towards the end of the first month of school, obtain specific input from the child's classroom teacher. Simply ask the teacher to provide, in writing, information about problems, concerns, and the child's strengths based on his or her observations of the child. (A specific form is not provided so that the teacher's observations are not colored or led by the content of the questions on such a form.)

5. Set a personal goal for each child. Decide on the child's personal goal for the pull-out lessons based on information obtained from the parents, feedback from the classroom teacher, and your own observation of the child. Personal goals help to individualize the program for each child. They usually identify areas of concern, which can be addressed in the sessions. For children with PDD, goals often fall into the categories of emotional regulation or increasing flexibility. In the area of emotional regulation, children with PDD often encounter two general types of issues: (a) anxiety and trouble with initiation and (b) anger and the need to control others.

6. The goal should be discussed with the child and written in the social skills notebook in the homework section. Progress should be discussed in each session. Once the goal is achieved, a new personal goal can be decided on. An example of a personal goal for a child who under-initiates is: "I will raise my hand in class and ask one question each day." A personal goal to increase the flexibility of a child who talks obsessively on his own topic might be, "Ask another person what he would like to talk about and listen to what he says."

Lesson Structure

There are 27 social skills pull-out lessons to be delivered as part of the S.O.S. program within each academic year. Children with PDD are pulled out of class for one hour per week for these lessons and seen in either group or individual sessions based on the criteria discussed in the Introduction on page 13. Children are grouped according to levels in language comprehension and expression. Language level is determined based on standardized language testing. S.O.S. pull-out lessons may be delivered by speech/language pathologists, guidance counselors, psychologists, or special education teachers trained in using the S.O.S. program.

Each social skills pull-out session adheres to the following format:

1. **Review of Personal Stories –** 15 minutes at the beginning of session
Each week all children receiving social skills lessons are asked to complete a graphic organizer in collaboration with their parents as part of their homework that tells a Personal Story (see page 70). A graphic organizer is a picture that shows the hierarchic organization for language. Specifically, it concretely and visually shows the main topic, subtopics, and lower-level details of the information the child will talk about. It makes clear that the main topic is more important than the subtopics and that subtopics are more important that lower-level details.

The child is taught to use the graphic organizer by first generating a topic sentence about the main topic (e.g., "I want to tell you a story."), then by generating a sentence about one subtopic (e.g., "Let me tell you what happened."), followed by the details attached to that subtopic, and then discussing the remainder of the subtopics and details in the same way. In drawing the graphic organizer for the Personal Story, the main topic goes in the circle in the middle of the page with the subtopics radiating out from there.

A Personal Story consists of three subtopics. The child and parents describe (a) a social situation that occurred, (b) the consequences of the child's actions (good or bad), and (c) what the child plans to do the next time a similar situation occurs. The Personal Story may deal with a difficult social situation or a social success. Particularly helpful are stories about a situation where the child correctly implemented a new social rule. Older children can fill in the graphic organizer on their own. Younger children's parents should fill in the organizer with them. For all children, parents should play a significant role in determining the content of the story. This gives them a chance to discuss both positive and negative social situations that have occurred with their child, to provide alternatives for inappropriate behavior if the child cannot think of what to do instead, and to reinforce appropriate social behaviors. (Graphic organizers are used many times throughout the curriculum to work on conversational skills and on sustaining an interaction.)

2. **Teaching a Social Rule –** 15- to 30-minute lesson
Children write information about the social rule in their social skills notebook according to the directions in the lesson. If the child cannot write, a handout containing the social rule is generated and provided. If a child can write but cannot write quickly enough, a handout may be provided that has part of the social rule written on it so the child only has to fill missing words into blanks. If a child typically uses a laptop and types all of his work, he should do the same in social skills sessions. Written rules should always be sent home in the notebook. The parents can audiotape the rule at home if this will be helpful to the child. (All rules are included in the Appendix.)

3. **Modeling and Role-Play –** 15-minute activity
This activity will vary, depending on the age and social proficiency of the children in the group. Typically, the social skills trainer demonstrates appropriate and inappropriate social behaviors

(implementation of the social rule in the lesson), as it is usually easier for the children to identify inappropriate behaviors when they are enacted by others. The children then role-play the appropriate behavior for practice.

4. Homework

At the end of each session, the teacher hands out the homework and makes sure the children put it in the homework section of the social skills notebook. Parents should be encouraged to do the homework with their child and to reinforce the social rules throughout the week. If there are questions for the child to answer as part of the homework, these should be written out on a separate sheet of paper. If a child has difficulty writing or cannot write, the parents may write the child's responses to the questions.

General Recommendations for Conducting Pull-Out Lessons

- Make sure all sessions emphasize turn taking.
- Use visual rather than solely auditory prompts.
- For children who cannot write, provide handouts with the social rule of the week. If a child typically uses a laptop to type in the classroom, this should be allowed in social skills sessions as well.
- Use context, including props and demonstrations specified in the lessons.
- Give children very direct feedback on their behavior.
- Decrease the directiveness as children's skill increases (emphasis on independence).
- Remember the goal is to provide appropriate alternate behaviors to substitute for inappropriate ones.
- Set firm limits with high expectations in a supportive environment.

Social Skills Lesson #1

STOP, THINK, GO #1

Goal:

To learn a strategy for emotional and behavioral modulation, including stopping inappropriate behaviors.

Materials

- blackboard and chalk*
- paper stoplights (these may be made or bought) – one with the red light colored in, one with the yellow light colored in, one with the green light colored in
- loose-leaf paper
- colored markers
- copies of handouts and homework
  Handout A, *STOP, THINK, GO* (p. 66)
  Handout B, *Rules for Behavior in Social Skills Lessons* (p. 67)
  Handout C, *Letter to Parents* (p. 68)
  Social Skills Homework: *STOP THINK GO #1*(p. 69)
  Graphic organizer for Personal Story (p. 70)

* Here and throughout, other writing surfaces and writing tools may be used as appropriate.

Note: Have students put handouts and other materials in the appropriate section of their notebooks after each lesson.

1. Talk about what will be happening in the social skills sessions (*learning social rules, practicing talking about things that happen with other children, etc.*).

2. Give children Handout A, *STOP, THINK and GO*. Show them the stoplights. Have them color the stoplights on the handout in the appropriate colors:

STOP	Don't do anything until you have a plan
THINK	Think of a plan
GO	Try the plan

Talk about what each step means. Chant the steps. Explain that before they do anything, they should stop and think.

3. Read children *"Jimmy Gets Too Silly"* (p. 64) while showing the cartoon strip (p. 65). (You may also act out the story to make the point clearer.) Talk about the importance of being able to stop; talk about the consequences for Jimmy when he did not stop.

4. Tell the children that the point of today's lesson is to understand the steps for learning appropriate behavior and to practice stopping.

5. On the board write out the rules for how to stop and have the children copy them:

> **RULE FOR STOPPING**
> * Take a deep breath.
> * Count to 10 slowly.
> * Say to myself, "I can stop."

6. Have the group practice stopping and going using the rules. Activities can include walking across the room, jumping, clapping.

7. Give the children Handout B, *Rules for Behavior in Social Skills Lessons*, and discuss them.

8. Hand out the letter to the parents, the homework, plus a blank graphic organizer for Personal Stories. Talk with the children about Personal Stories and how they will fill in the Personal Story graphic organizer each week with their parents and bring it to the next session.

STOP, THINK, GO is adapted *from Social Star: General Interaction Skills (Book 1)*, page 66, by N. Gajewski, P. Hirn, and P. Mayo (Eau Claire, WI: Thinking Publications, 1993). Used with permission.

"Jimmy Gets Too Silly"

One day in gym class the kids were running races. They had to run from one side of the gym to the other, touch the wall, and run back. When it was Jimmy's turn, he started to run. He slipped and fell, and all of the kids started to laugh; Jimmy laughed the hardest. Jimmy got up but instead of running, he decided to fall down again and again. The teacher told him to stop falling down and to start running the race. But Jimmy just kept falling down and laughing. The other kids stopped laughing but Jimmy kept laughing, falling down, and then rolling on the floor. The gym teacher was so angry that he sent Jimmy to the principal's office.

Jimmy Gets Too Silly

STOP 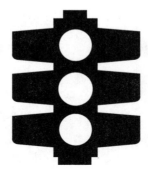 **Don't do anything until you have a plan**

THINK  **Think of a plan**

GO 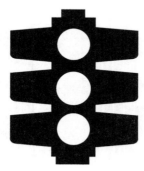 **Try the plan**

RULES FOR BEHAVIOR IN SOCIAL SKILLS LESSONS

1. LISTEN

2. WORK HARD

3. BE KIND

**CONTROL YOURSELF –
YOU HAVE THE POWER
TO DO SO**
**(Adults will help you, but <u>you</u>
are the one who controls
your behavior)**

Handout C, Lesson #1

(School Letterhead)

Dear Parents,

I would like to introduce myself as your child's social skills trainer for the coming year. I will be teaching your child's pull-out social skills lessons for one hour per week. I will also train and supervise your child's peer mentors. Each week you will receive (in your child's social skills notebook) a homework sheet with work intended to reinforce the social skills lesson of the week. Please do the homework *with* your child. Discuss the answers to questions and have your child write his answers on the homework sheet. (If your child has difficulty writing, you may write the answers to the homework questions.) Please practice the social rules you find in your child's notebook throughout each week. By doing the homework with your child, you help your child generalize these new skills to other situations, and you help make the skills automatic. Our partnership makes it possible for your child to make gains that cannot be made if either you or I work with him or her alone.

In addition to other activities, each week you will be asked to write a Personal Story with your child and make sure he/she brings it back to school for the next lesson. You will do this by filling in the attached graphic organizer. You can do the writing, but do it *with* your child. Choose any one social situation that occurs during this week.

The Personal Story should include three parts:
- a description of a difficult social situation where your child experienced trouble behaving appropriately (OR a description of a good social choice made by your child)
- a description of the consequences of that behavior
- other options for behavior the next time a similar situation arises

I look forward to working with you to help your child to have a very successful year in social skills.

During the school year, parent meetings will be set up to discuss the program. I will let you know when and where the meetings will take place. I look forward to seeing you there. If you need to reach me, my e-mail address is _____.   The office phone is _____. The best way to reach me is e-mail.

Sincerely,

SOCIAL SKILLS HOMEWORK #1:
STOP, THINK, GO #1

Dear Parents,

Today we learned about rules for appropriate behavior, especially stopping.

1. If you have not yet obtained one, please make sure your child gets a loose-leaf notebook. This will serve as the social skills notebook. Please fill the notebook with loose-leaf paper and put dividers in to make three sections (the first will be the class work section, the second will be the homework section, and the third will be the section we use to communicate with each other). This book will not only be used for lesson materials, it will also provide a way in which I, your child's social skills teacher, the classroom teacher, and you will communicate about your child's social skills.

2. Write a Personal Story (use the graphic organizer attached) *with* your child about something that happens between sessions. A letter providing the details of how to do this is also being sent to you.

3. Review the rules below for stopping and practice with your child.

   RULE FOR STOPPING
   - Take a deep breath.
   - Count to 10 slowly.
   - Say to myself, "I can stop." I can _____ instead.

4. Review the rules of conduct for social skills sessions (see Handout B in notebook).

What happened?

_____

_____

_____

_____

My Personal Story

Consequences?

_____

_____

_____

_____

What should you do next time?

_____

_____

_____

_____

Social Skills Lesson #2

STOP, THINK, GO #2

Goal:

To review the strategy for emotional modulation and stopping inappropriate behaviors and to give the children practice.

Materials

- blackboard and chalk
- paper stoplights
- loose-leaf paper
- tape recorder
- music tapes
- copies of handouts and homework
  Handout A, *Empty Description Graphic Organizer About Child* (p. 73)
  Handout B, *Sample Description Organizer About Child Using Pictures* (p. 74)
  Social Skills Homework: *STOP, THINK, GO #2* (p. 75)
  Graphic organizer for Personal Stories (p. 76)

Note: Make sure students put handouts and other materials in the appropriate section of their notebooks after each lesson.

1. Review homework.

2. Go over the Personal Stories, discussing other options for behavior in the given situations (with older students focus on the consequences of actions – how one's actions affect others and oneself). You may go over each child's story briefly, or you can choose one that provides an important lesson for the entire group and go over it in more detail.

3. Talk about the purpose of the lesson (*to practice stopping and controlling behavioral reactions to strong emotions and inappropriate social behaviors*).

4. Play the following stop-and-go games:
   - freeze tag
   - musical chairs
   - freeze dance
   - 1... 2 ... 3 ... red light
   - running in circles

Have the students run in circles around you and stop when you give the cue as follows.

At first use the red and green stoplights to visually cue stopping and going. Then use verbal cues or nonverbal auditory cues such as a clap or finger snap. Later, use more subtle visuals such as facial expressions that indicate it is time to stop. (The idea is to allow the children to start to lose control with silliness and then regain control when given various cues; work in the future will focus on emotions like anger and anxiety.) Make sure they regain control by taking a deep breath, counting to 10, or whispering "I can stop."

5. Give out homework, including both graphic organizers, and remind the children to bring it back the next lesson. *(This is done at the end of each lesson.)*

Description Organizer About Child

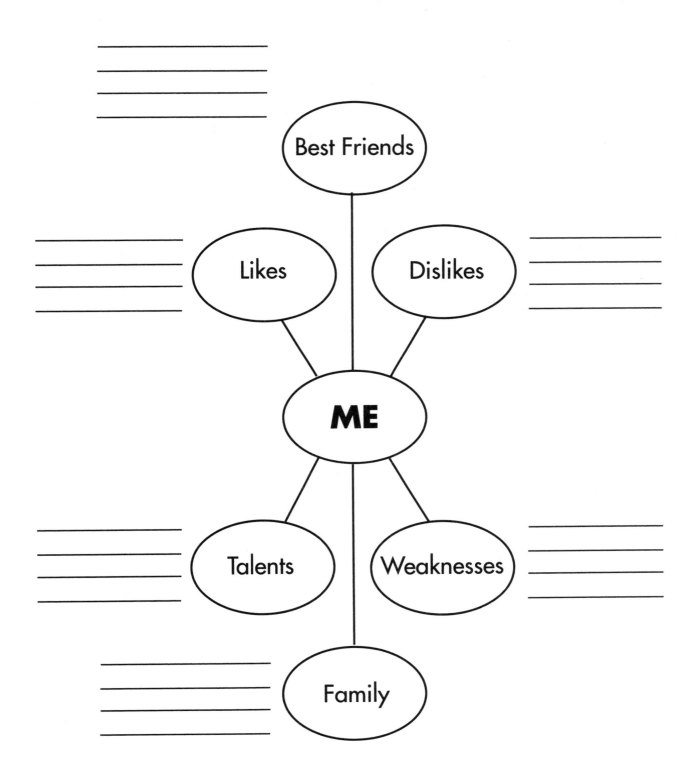

Sample Description Organizer
Using Pictures

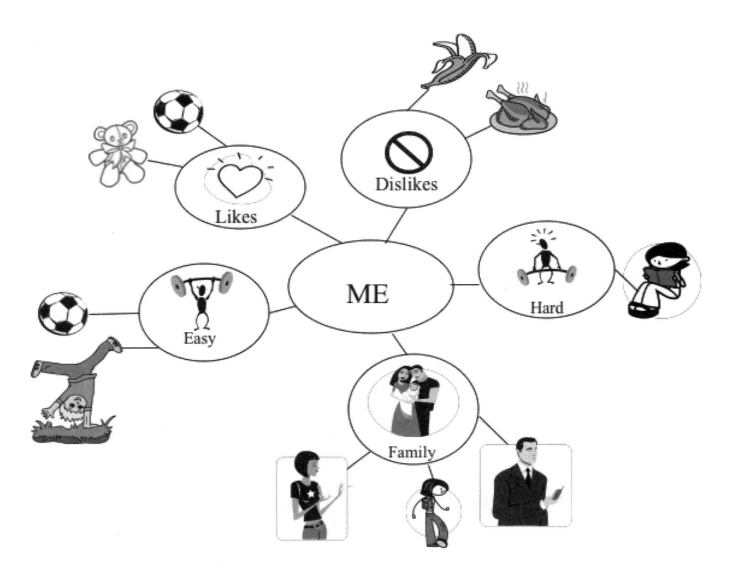

This graphic organizer was created with Kidspiration® (© 2004) Inspiration Software, Inc.

SOCIAL SKILLS HOMEWORK #2:
STOP, THINK, GO #2

Dear Parents,

Today we practiced using the rules for appropriate behavior, especially for stopping.

1. On the attached sheet, fill in the Personal Story graphic organizer *with* your child about something that happened between sessions. The Personal Story should include the following parts: (a) a description of a difficult social situation your child experienced or a difficulty your child had with appropriate behavior or a description of a good social choice made by your child; (b) a description of the consequences of that behavior; and (c) other options for behavior the next time a similar situation arises.

2. Please review the stopping strategy.
    Specifically,

    RULE FOR STOPPING
    *   Take a deep breath.
    *   Count to 10 slowly.
    *   Say to myself, "I can stop." I can _____ instead.

2. Practice getting silly and then stopping using the "HOW DO I STOP?" strategy. Run around with your child or engage in a fun activity during which your child may get too silly. When s/he starts to get silly, cue her/him to use the stopping strategy (by saying "stop," snapping your fingers or sending a certain look).

3. Talk with your child about times when it is difficult to stop.
    *   Make a list of situations in which it is hard for your child to stop. Put it in the social skills notebook.
    *   Decide on one situation in particular to work on using the strategies learned and make improvement in this area a personal goal for your child. Put a note in the notebook to let me know which goal you have chosen to work on.

4. Start filling in the attached autobiographical graphic organizer (description organizer) with your child. In this case the main topic is your child's name. Subtopics go in the circles that radiate out from the center circle. Your child's subtopics should include likes (favorite TV show, movie, teacher, subject, etc.), dislikes, strengths, weaknesses, family. It may also include pets, hobbies, recent family trips, etc. (Nonreaders or early readers should use pictures with words in their organizers. For example, you can draw a picture to represent each word. If you have a dog as a pet, draw a little picture of it and write the dog's name beneath the picture.)

Personal Story Organizer

What happened?

_____
_____
_____
_____

My Personal Story

Consequences?

_____
_____
_____
_____

What should you do next time?

_____
_____
_____
_____

Social Skills Lesson #3
INTERRUPTING APPROPRIATELY
Goals:

To learn to interrupt appropriately. To understand situations when it is and is not appropriate to interrupt.

Materials

- blackboard and chalk
- paper stoplight
- loose-leaf paper
- markers
- copies of handouts and homework
  Handout A, *Interrupting comic strip* (p. 79)
  Handout B, *Role-Playing* (p. 80)
  Social Skills Homework #3: *Interrupting Appropriately* (p. 81)
  Graphic organizer for Personal Story (p. 82)

Note: Make sure students put handouts and other materials in the appropriate section of their notebooks after each lesson.

1. Review homework.

2. Go over Personal Stories, discussing other options for behavior in the situation (with older students focus on consequences of actions – how one's actions affect others and oneself).

3. Talk about the purpose of the lesson (*learning the steps for interrupting appropriately; deciding if it is a good time to interrupt or if it can wait*).

4. Write out the rules for interrupting on the blackboard. Have the children copy. Remind the kids that before they do anything, they need to stop and think.

RULES FOR INTERRUPTING APPROPRIATELY
- STOP
- THINK (What is the appropriate way to interrupt? Is it a good time to interrupt?) If yes,
- GO!

Get the person's attention (Say, "excuse me"; stand where the person can see you and look at him or her. When the person looks at you, say "excuse me.")

Say you are sorry for interrupting

Tell why you are interrupting

Talk about the steps for interrupting appropriately. Give the children the cartoon strip (Handout A) to illustrate the point. Act out the steps.

5. Practice by role-playing the following situations. (*Note:* It is helpful to use props. Also, the children often enjoy role-playing more if it is done like a game show with a bell sound for a correct role-play and a buzzer sound for an incorrect role-play. Demonstrate interrupting correctly and incorrectly in each situation, having the children make the game show sounds. Then have each child practice the *correct* way to interrupt.)
   * Teacher working at desk; child needs help with work.
   * Teacher talking to principal; child needs help with work.
   * Teacher talking to principal; child needs to tell about other child hurt on playground.
   * Mom on phone; child wants snack.
   * Kids talking in hall; child wants to join conversation.
   * Kids talking quietly in a corner; serious faces, child wants to join.
   * Teacher teaching in front of class; child has a question about the work.
   Note: Tell the children that interrupting is always okay if there is an emergency (if someone is sick or in danger).

6. Give the children copies of Handout B. After role-playing pick one or two situations and fill in the thought bubbles.

7. Discuss other issues related to interrupting. Point out that one interruption may be fine but that repeated interruptions are usually a problem. Discuss "How many interruptions are too many?," "How many questions about the work during class time are too many?," and so on. What should a child do if he has already asked too many questions and still does not understand the work? (If these are issues for the children in your group, have them write out the answers.)

8. **REVIEW:**
   * STOP, THINK, GO (chant)
   * HOW DO I STOP?
     - Take a deep breath.
     - Count to 10 slowly.
     - Say to myself, "I can stop."

9. Hand out homework, including blank graphic organizer.

STOP AND THINK

Get the person's attention

Say you are sorry for interrupting

Tell why you are interrupting

**STOP
AND
THINK**

**Get the
person's
attention**

**Say you are
sorry for
interrupting**

**Tell why
you are
interrupting**

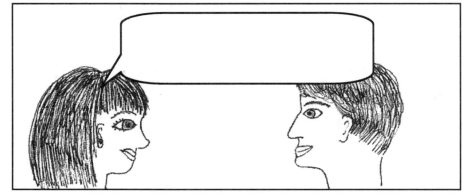

Social Skills Homework #3:
INTERRUPTING APPROPRIATELY

Dear Parents,

Today we learned about rules for interrupting appropriately – how to do it and how to judge when it is appropriate.

1. Write a Personal Story (use the graphic organizer) *with* your child about something that happens between sessions. The Personal Story should include the following parts: (a) a description of a difficult social situation your child experienced or a difficulty your child had with appropriate behavior (or a description of a good social choice made by your child); (b) a description of the consequences of that behavior; (c) other options for behavior the next time a similar situation arises.

2. Please review the work in your child's notebook. Practice interrupting appropriately. As situations come up during the week, review the circumstances under which it would be inappropriate and when it would be appropriate to interrupt.

Child's Homework

Please answer the following questions. Write your answers on a separate sheet of paper. Do this with one of your parents. (*Parents, remember if your child has difficulty writing the responses, you may write them in.*)

1. Patrick is looking for a book about Saturn in the library and needs help. The librarian is helping another student. Should he interrupt or wait? Why?

   Patrick is still looking for a book about Saturn in the library and still needs help. The librarian is behind her desk working at the computer. Should he interrupt or wait? Why?

2. Dan feels sick to his stomach and needs to go to the bathroom. His teacher is talking to another student. Should he interrupt or wait? Why?

3. Finish the graphic organizer about yourself started in Lesson #2.

What
happened?

_____
_____
_____
_____

**My Personal
Story**

Consequences?

_____
_____
_____
_____

What should
you do next
time?

_____
_____
_____
_____

Social Skills Lesson #4
CONVERSATIONS: PARTS 1 & 4 – GREETINGS AND CLOSINGS

Goals:

To learn how to greet others appropriately and close interactions appropriately.

Materials

- blackboard and chalk
- stoplights
- loose-leaf paper
- markers
- mirror
- copies of handouts and homework
  Handout A, *Greetings* (p. 85)
  Handout B, *Small Talk* (p. 86)
  Handout C, *The Main Point* (p. 87)
  Handout D, *Closings* (p. 88)
  Social Skills Homework: *Conversations: Parts 1 & 4 – Greetings and Closings* (p. 89)
  Graphic organizer for Personal Story (p. 90)

Note: Make sure students put handouts and other materials in the appropriate section of their notebooks after each lesson.

1. Review homework.

2. Go over Personal Stories, discussing other options for behavior in the situation (with older students focus on consequences of actions – how one's actions affect others and oneself).

3. Talk about the purpose of the lesson (*understanding how to greet others and understanding how to close an interaction appropriately*). Put up the parts of a conversation strip on the wall. Give each child the four handouts that make up the conversation strip. Have them read the frames of the strip that correspond to greetings and closings.

4. Write out the rules for greetings on the board and have the children copy them.

> **RULES FOR GREETINGS**
> - STOP
> - THINK (Is this person familiar? How do I greet appropriately?)
> - GO
>   - Make eye contact.
>   - Have a friendly face.
>   - Say hi, or hello," or "good to see you." (with the person's name if you know it)

5. Demonstrate friendly and unfriendly faces and have the children tell which kind of face you are making.

6. Have the children look in the mirror and practice making friendly faces.

7. Have the children line up outside the classroom door and come in practicing greetings.

8. Write out the rules for closings on the blackboard and have the children copy them.

> **RULES FOR CLOSINGS**
> - STOP
> - THINK (Is this person familiar? How do I greet appropriately?)
> - GO
>   - Make eye contact.
>   - Have a friendly face.
>   - Say "good-bye" or "see you later." (with the person's name if you know it)

9. Demonstrate appropriate and inappropriate closings and have the children tell you which are appropriate and which are inappropriate and why.

10. Have the children line up in the class and practice closings as they leave the room.

11. Have the children come back in. Explain that appropriate greetings and closings will now be part of every session and that they should use them in other situations as well. Talk about the idea that if we have a friendly face and use greetings, others think were nice and like us.

12. With older children talk about situations in school when it would be inappropriate to greet (e.g., greeting the principal when he is busy talking to someone; greeting anyone in class when the teacher is giving a lesson).

13. Hand out homework, including blank graphic organizer.

Handout C, Lesson #4
MAIN POINT

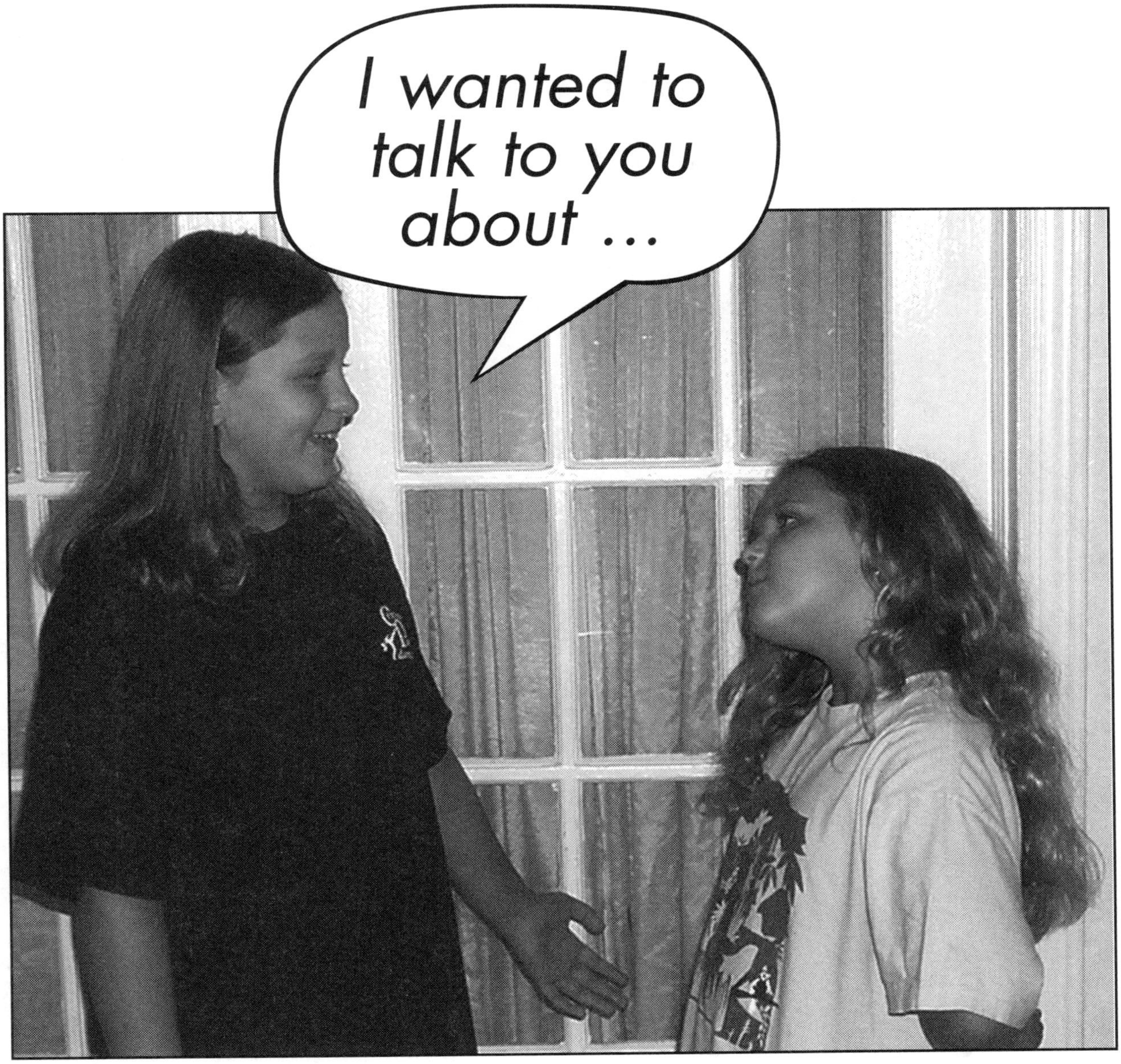

Social Skills Homework #4:
CONVERSATIONS:
Parts 1 & 4—Greetings and Closings

Dear Parents,

Today we learned about rules for greetings and closings in conversations.

1. Write a Personal Story (use the graphic organizer) *with* your child about something that happens between sessions. The Personal Story should include the following parts: (a) a description of a difficult social situation your child experienced or a difficulty your child had with appropriate behavior or a description of a good social choice made by your child; (b) a description of the consequences of that behavior; (c) other options for behavior the next time a similar situation arises.

2. Please review the work in your child's notebook. Practice greetings and closings in conversations.

Child's Homework

Please answer the following questions. Write your answers on a separate sheet of paper. Do this with one of your parents. (*Parents, remember if your child has difficulty writing the responses, you may write them in.*)

1. What is the first thing you should do when starting an interaction? Why?

2. Why shouldn't you greet complete strangers if your parents (or another trusted adult) are not around to say it's O.K.?

3. What should you do when you are leaving someone you were talking with or playing with? Why?

4. Draw a picture of what your face should look like when you greet someone you know.

Personal Story Organizer

What
happened?

_____
_____
_____
_____

**My Personal
Story**

Consequences?

_____
_____
_____
_____

What should
you do next
time?

_____
_____
_____
_____

Social Skills Lesson #5

INITIATING INTERACTIONS

Goals:

To learn to initiate a reciprocal interaction appropriately. Understanding if it is a good time to start an interaction.

Materials

- blackboard and chalk
- stoplights
- loose-leaf paper
- markers
- copies of handouts and homework
  Handout A, *Starting an Interaction* (p. 93)
  Handout B, *Graphic Organizer of Good and Bad Times to Initiate* (p. 94)
  Social Skills Homework: *Initiating Interactions* (p. 95)
  Graphic organizer for Personal Story (p. 96)

Note: Make sure students put handouts and other materials in the appropriate section of their notebooks after each lesson.

1. Review homework.

2. Go over Personal Stories, discussing other options for behavior in the situation (with older students focus on consequences of actions – how one's actions affect others and oneself).

3. Talk about the purpose of the lesson (*understanding how to initiate an interaction, deciding if it is a good time to initiate an interaction*).

4. Write out the rules for initiating an interaction and have the children copy them.

RULES FOR INITIATING AN INTERACTION
- STOP
- THINK (is it a good time to initiate an interaction?) If yes,
- GO!
  - Make eye contact
  - Have a friendly face
  - Say hi (If you know the person, say his name; if you don't know the person, introduce yourself. Say, "My name is_____; what's yours?")
  - THINK: What is the person doing? Do I want to join the person? Is it a good time?
  - THINK: Should I start a conversation, play with the person, or wait until later?
  - GO (Say, "What are you doing?"; "Can I join you?" "Can I play too?")

(For older children, also address initiation on the telephone. Use play telephones as props.)

---

5. Give the students Handout A and discuss their observations of the two girls in the picture, one of whom is initiating an interaction with the other.

6. Role-play situations such as the following:
   - Good time to join for play (e.g., kids playing catch or tag)
   - Good time to join for conversation (e.g., kids talking about a lesson you were in or about a fieldtrip you went on)
   - Bad time to start play or conversation (e.g., children enter class, teacher says it's time to sit down and get started)
   - Bad time to try to get into a game (e.g., checkers game in progress)
   - Bad time to start a conversation (e.g., ball game/running game starting up or in progress)
   Make sure to discuss that it is important to stop and think before starting an interaction. Use the stoplight to cue children to stop and think if they need that cues.

7. Discuss how you know if it is a good time or not to initiate interaction. Give the children a copy of Handout B and ask them to fill in the graphic organizer of good and bad times to initiate.

8. Point out that when you initiate an interaction, the other person may not want to talk or play. Tell the children that it's OK and that they should say, "OK maybe another time."

9. **REVIEW:**
   - STOP, THINK, GO (chant)
   - HOW DO I STOP?
     - Take a deep breath.
     - Count to 10 slowly.
     - Say to myself, "I can stop."

10. Hand out homework, including blank graphic organizer.

DESCRIPTION ORGANIZER:
Good Times and Bad Times to Initiate

```
   ⬭
GOOD TIMES          _____
                    _____
                    _____
                    _____
                    _____
   ▭                _____
INITIATING

   ⬭
BAD TIMES           _____
                    _____
                    _____
                    _____
                    _____
```

Social Skills Homework #5: INITIATING INTERACTIONS

Dear Parents,

Today we learned about rules for initiating interactions, how to do it, how to judge when it is an appropriate time to do it, and how to continue the interaction if appropriate. It will take time and practice for your child to effectively continue play and conversational interactions.

1. Write a Personal Story (use the graphic organizer) *with* your child about something that happens between sessions. The Personal Story should include the following parts: (a) a description of a difficult social situation your child experienced or a difficulty your child had with appropriate behavior (or a description of a good social choice made by your child); (b) a description of the consequences of that behavior; (c) other options for behavior the next time a similar situation arises.

2. Please review the work in your child's notebook. Practice initiating an interaction. As situations come up during the week, discuss whether it would be a good idea to initiate an interaction with particular people and review the circumstances under which it would be inappropriate to continue the interaction.

Child's Homework

- Join in an activity with one of your parents or a sister or brother. Follow the rules for initiating interactions. Maybe you could join your mom to help make dinner or maybe you could suggest playing a board game with family members.

What happened?

_____
_____
_____
_____

My Personal Story

Consequences?

_____
_____
_____
_____

What should you do next time?

_____
_____
_____
_____

Social Skills Lesson #6

ASKING FOR HELP

Goal:

To learn how to ask for help when needed and in an appropriate way.

Materials

- blackboard and chalk
- loose-leaf paper
- markers
- copies of handouts and homework
  Social Skills Homework: *Asking for Help* (p. 99)
  Graphic organizer for Personal Story (p. 100)

Note: Make sure students put handouts and other materials in the appropriate section of their notebooks after each lesson.

1. Review homework.

2. Go over Personal Stories, discussing other options for behavior in the situation (with older students focus on consequences of actions – how one's actions affect others and oneself).

3. Talk about the purpose of the lesson (*learning the steps for asking for help*).

4. Write out the rules for asking for help and have the children copy them.

RULES FOR ASKING FOR HELP
- STOP
- THINK (do I need help or should I keep trying myself?)
  - If you really need help,
- GO!
  - Interrupt appropriately
  - Clearly say what you need help with
  - Listen
  - If you do not understand, patiently ask questions
  - Say thank you

---

5. Practice asking for help by role-playing the following situations:
   - The class is in the middle of math. You drop your pencil, and it rolls away. Ask for help to get the pencil back.
   - You didn't write down all of the spelling words before you went home and you need to get them so you can study for the test. How do you get help?
   - You really want to play a game that some other kids know how to play but you don't. How can you get help?
   - You are reading a great book but you don't know some of the words. The boy who sits next to you is a good reader. How can you get help?

6. Talk about peer mentors. Discuss who they are and what they do. Point out that they are the children to ask for help on the playground. Write down the two jobs of peer mentors:
   - to help the kids join in at lunch and on the playground
   - to help resolve conflicts

7. Hand out the homework, including a blank graphic organizer.

Social Skills Homework #6:
ASKING FOR HELP

Dear Parents,

Today we learned about rules for asking for help from others.

1. Write a Personal Story (use the graphic organizer) *with* your child about the play date that is part of this homework.

2. Please review the work in your child's notebook.

3. Set up a play date for your child with one other child. Make this a structured play date with a set time limit. First offer a snack, then have the children do a simple craft or activity together. You might buy two craft kits. Have the children complete one kit at a time. One child helps the other first, and then the second child helps the first child. Emphasize that the person being helped determines the amount of help needed and that helping is not controlling. That is, the person helping can make suggestions but the person being helped makes the decisions about the project. After the projects are finished, encourage the children to spend a little time playing a video game or playing catch. Then the play date ends.

What happened?

_____
_____
_____
_____

My Personal Story

Consequences?

_____
_____
_____
_____

What should you do next time?

_____
_____
_____
_____

Social Skills Lesson #7

OFFERING HELP

Goal:

To learn how to offer help when needed in an appropriate way.

Materials

- blackboard and chalk
- loose-leaf paper
- markers
- building blocks
- your instructions for building a house
- copies of handouts and homework
  Social Skills Homework: *Offering Help* (p.103)
  Graphic organizer for Personal Story (p.104)

Note: Make sure students put handouts and other materials in the appropriate section of their notebooks after each lesson.

1. Review homework.

2. Go over Personal Stories, discussing other options for behavior in the situation (with older students focus on consequences of actions – how one's actions affect others and oneself).

3. Talk about the purpose of the lesson (*learning the steps for giving help*).

4. Write out the rules for giving help and have children copy them.

RULES FOR GIVING HELP
- STOP
- THINK (Did the person ask for help or did the person say YES when I asked, "Can I help you?")
- GO!
  - Listen to what the person needs.
  - If you do not understand, patiently ask questions.
  - Help if you can OR find someone who can help.

---

5. Play a block building game. Seat the children at a table and tell them they are not allowed to move from their spot for the whole game. Give one child (the foreman) instructions for building a house (give the child written instructions or whisper instructions to the child). Put the blocks necessary to build the house near a second child (the supplier), out of reach of the others. Make a third child the builder. The goal is to end up with a house that fits the description in the instructions. The children should be coached to ask for help and give help to each other as needed. This activity fosters *joint attention* (i.e., helps all children to attend to the same thing at the same time) and reinforces the rules for giving and getting help.

   (*Note:* Specific instructions depend on available materials. An example would be to build a house that is blue on the bottom, red in the middle, and has a green roof.)

6. Hand out homework, including a blank graphic organizer.

Social Skills Homework #7:
OFFERING HELP

Dear Parents,

Today we learned about rules for offering help to others.

1. Write a Personal Story (use the graphic organizer) *with* your child about the play date that is part of this homework.

2. Please review the work in your child's notebook.

3. Set up a second play date. Again, orchestrate a simple craft where one child helps the other first, and then the second child helps the first child. Emphasize the rules for helping. Remind the children that the "owner" of the project makes the decisions, whereas the helper asks how the owner wants the project done and wants the helper to help. Play dates are extremely important for developing social skills.

Child's Homework

Please answer the following questions. Write your answers on a separate sheet of paper. Do this with one of your parents. (*Parents, remember if your child has difficulty writing the responses, you may write them in.*)

- If a person does not want your help, should you help? Why or why not?

Personal Story Organizer

What happened?

_____
_____
_____
_____

My Personal Story

Consequences?

_____
_____
_____
_____

What should you do next time?

_____
_____
_____
_____

Social Skills Lesson #8

PLAYGROUND SURVIVAL #1

Goal:

To learn and practice age-appropriate playground games.

Materials

- blackboard and chalk
- loose-leaf paper
- markers, balls, etc., for playground games
- copies of handouts and homework
  Social Skills Homework: *Playground Survival #1* (p. 106)
  Graphic organizer for Personal Story (p. 107)

Note: Make sure students put handouts and other materials in the appropriate section of their notebooks after each lesson.

1. Review homework.

2. Go over Personal Stories, discussing other options for behavior in the situation (with older students focus on consequences of actions – how one's actions affect others and oneself).

3. Talk about the purpose of the lesson (*learning what to do on the playground*).

4. Throughout this lesson, talk about how peer mentors will be there to help the children on the playground.

5. Make a list with the children of the kinds of games they see the other children play; have each child write the list in his or her notebook.

6. Choose games from the list generated by the children or common games such as kickball, tag, or hopscotch. Go out to the playground and teach the games. The purpose of this lesson is to teach the children the rules for various playground games and give them an opportunity to practice with each other.

7. Write in two games that peers play during recess on the homework sheets so that the children can practice these for homework.

8. Hand out homework, including a blank graphic organizer.

Social Skills Homework #8:
PLAYGROUND SURVIVAL #1

Dear Parents,

Today we reviewed and learned rules for how to play a variety of playground games.

1. Write a Personal Story (use the graphic organizer) *with* your child about something that happens between sessions.

2. Please review the work in your child's notebook.

3. Please practice playing the following games with your child:

_____

_____

Personal Story Organizer

What happened?

_____
_____
_____
_____

My Personal Story

Consequences?

_____
_____
_____
_____

What should you do next time?

_____
_____
_____
_____

Social Skills Lesson #9

PLAYGROUND SURVIVAL #2

Goal:

To learn rules for how to join and stay in games on the playground.

Materials

- blackboard and chalk
- loose-leaf paper markers
- copies of handouts and homework
  Handout A, *Ways to Initiate with Other Kids and Stay in the Game* (p. 110)
  Handout B, *Ways to Initiate with Other Kids and Stay in the Game* (p. 111)
  Social Skills Homework: *Playground Survival #2* (p. 112)
  Graphic organizer for Personal Story (p. 113)

Note: Make sure students put handouts and other materials in the appropriate section of their notebooks each lesson.

1. Review homework.

2. Go over Personal Stories, discussing other options for behavior in the situation (with older students focus on consequences of actions – how one's actions affect others and oneself).

3. Talk about the purpose of the lesson (*learning more about what to do on the playground*).

4. PEER MENTORS START ON THE PLAYGROUND THIS WEEK! Throughout this lesson talk about how peer mentors are there to help the children on the playground. Tell the kids that peer mentors will ask them to play. If they don't know how to play a game, they are to ask for help; the peer mentors will teach them. Explain that once they start playing a game, it is important to use the rules for staying in a game.

5. Write out rules for staying in a game and have children copy.

RULES FOR STAYING IN A GAME	
DO	**DON'T**
• Let others into your game	• Cry or whine
• Follow the rules	• Try to take control
• Win or lose – be a good sport	• Push, hit
• Compliment other kids ("That was great!")	• Disrupt (wreck) the game
• Share and take turns ("Would you like a turn?"; "Your turn"; "What do you want to play?")	
• Play safe – if it gets too rough, walk away	

6. Explain to the students that they can ask their mentors or other kids to play too. Write out the rules for joining in and have children copy them.

RULES FOR JOINING IN (IF YOU ARE READY)

DO
- Ask "Can I play?"
- Ask "What can I do?"
- Make sure you know the rules of the game
- Suggest what you can do in the group
- Make a plan with someone ahead of time
- Say something nice

DON'T
- Push, hit
- Brag
- Disagree with the group
- Just walk around
- Control the game
- Disrupt (wreck) the game
- Only talk about you
- Fool around

Tell the children that they may not feel ready to join in with other kids on the playground yet. That's O.K. They should just practice joining in (through role-play) with the help of their parents and teachers.

7. With older children, discuss open groups and closed groups. "Open groups" are groups of people where any number of people can interact and play. In "closed groups," interaction is limited to a certain number of individuals by the activity in which the members of the group are engaged. An example of a closed group is two children playing checkers. Explain that with a closed group, it may be O.K. to watch the game and ask to play in the next game.

8. Discuss that *all* children are rejected sometimes (between 30 and 70 percent of the time). Emphasize that it is a good idea to keep trying to join in. Talk about what children can do if they cannot get into a group one day. They can say "O.K., maybe next time."

9. To practice, give the students Handouts A and B and help them fill in the bubbles with appropriate things to say to initiate with other kids (A) and to stay in the game (B).

10. Hand out homework, including a blank graphic organizer.

Handout A, Lesson #9
Ways to Initiate with Other Kids and Stay in the Game

by Barbara Wygoda

1.   What would you say to join a game?

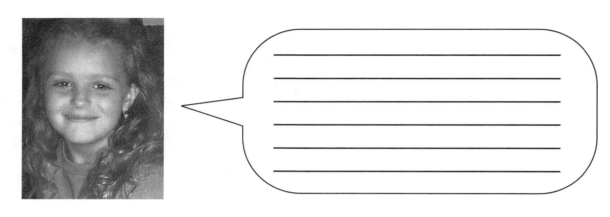

2.   Make a plan to play with someone later. What do you say?

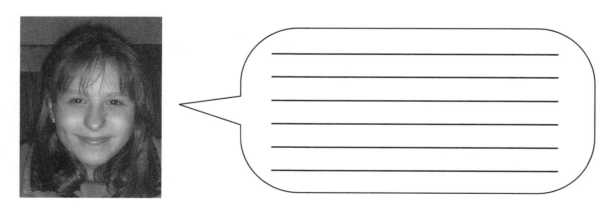

Handout B, Lesson #9
Ways to Initiate with Other Kids and Stay in the Game

by Barbara Wygoda

1. **Tell your teammates something nice during the game.**

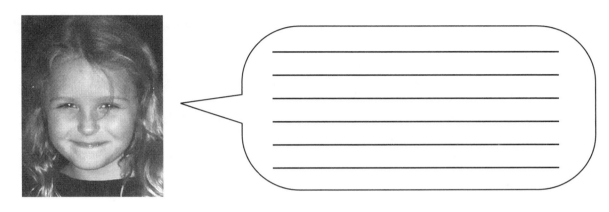

2. **Tell/ask your teammates what you could do in the game.**

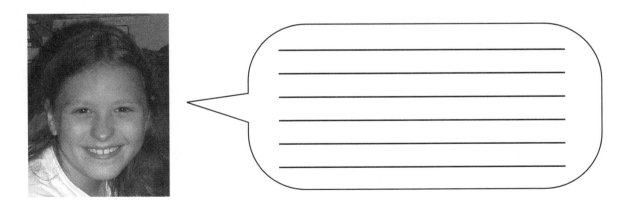

Social Skills Homework #9:
PLAYGROUND SURVIVAL #2

Dear Parents,

Today we learned about rules for how to join in and stay in activities on the playground.

1. Write a Personal Story (use the graphic organizer) *with* your child about something that happened between sessions.

2. Please review the work in your child's notebook.

3. Go to a playground and sit on a bench with your child. Watch children play. Talk about what you both see. For example, how do the children enter games? How do they stay in the games?

Child's Homework

1. Make a "don't" sign (like "no ghosts" in *Ghostbusters*). Inside the sign write all the playground don'ts.

2. Make a set of cardboard circles. Punch holes in them. Write one playground "do" on the front of each circle. Hang them on string and put them up in your room.

What
happened?

_____

_____

_____

_____

My Personal Story

Consequences?

_____

_____

_____

_____

What should
you do next
time?

_____

_____

_____

_____

Social Skills Lesson #10

BEING A FRIEND

Goal:

To learn rules for becoming a good friend, including compliments, helpfulness, and turn taking.

Materials

- blackboard and chalk
- loose-leaf paper
- markers
- jump rope
- basketball
- copies of handouts and homework
  Social Skills Homework: *Being a Good Friend* (p. 116)
  Graphic organizer for Personal Story (p. 117)

Note: Make sure students put handouts and other materials in the appropriate section of their notebooks after each lesson.

1. Review homework.

2. Go over Personal Stories, discussing other options for behavior in the situation (with older students focus on consequences of actions – how one's actions affect others and oneself).

3. Talk about the purpose of the lesson (*how to be a good friend*).

4. Define friendship. On the board write out the children's ideas about the meaning of friendship. Decide on a definition and have the children write it in their notebooks.

5. Write the following and have children copy:

RULES FOR BECOMING A GOOD FRIEND
- Give compliments ("Good job," "Great idea," or when someone is upset, "It's O.K.," etc.)
- Smile
- Be helpful
- Take turns – let your friends have their way sometimes

---

6. Discuss "put-downs" and compliments. Make a list on the board of nice things the children can say to each other. Encourage them to give each other a "pat on the back" on a regular basis.

7. Explain that when people feel good about themselves when they are with you, they want to be your friend. (Point out that words are powerful. Compliments make people feel good. If you compliment someone, he/she will feel good around you and want to be with you.)

8. Play a game where the children take turns doing things such as dribble a basketball, jump rope, hop on one foot (if the children get over-excited, it is an opportunity to review stopping). Tell the children that you will be watching for compliments during the activity, as well as smiles and help-fulness.

9. Hand out homework, including a blank graphic organizer

Social Skills Homework #10:
Being a Good Friend

Dear Parents,

Today we learned about rules for becoming a good friend.

1. Write a Personal Story (use the graphic organizer) *with* your child about something that happens between sessions.

2. Please review the work in your child's notebook. Talk about the secret of friendship and how it works. Give examples from your own life.

Child's Homework

Please answer the following questions. Write your answers on a separate sheet of paper. Do this with one of your parents. (*Parents, remember, if your child has difficulty writing the responses, you may write them in.*)

1. What are the things you can do to become a good friend?

2. Why should you tell the truth when you give compliments?

3. If your friend asks you to do something that you know is wrong, should you do it?

What
happened?

_____
_____
_____
_____

**My Personal
Story**

Consequences?

_____
_____
_____
_____

What should
you do next
time?

_____
_____
_____
_____

Social Skills Lesson #11

YOUR BODY SPEAKS TOO – EYES, BODY POSITION, PROXIMITY

Goal:

To learn rules for appropriate eye contact, body position, and proximity.

Materials

- blackboard and chalk
- loose-leaf paper
- markers
- copies of handouts and homework
  Social Skills Homework: *Your Body Speaks – Eyes, Body Position, Proximity* (p.120)
  Graphic organizer for Personal Story (p.121)

Note: Make sure students put handouts and other materials in the appropriate section of their notebooks after each lesson.

1. Review homework.

2. Go over Personal Stories, discussing other options for behavior in the situation (with older students focus on consequences of actions – how one's actions affect others and oneself).

3. Talk about the purpose of the lesson (*making good eye contact, having good body posture*).

4. Demonstrate poor eye contact: (a) never looking and (b) staring.

5. Demonstrate good eye contact: looking most of the time but not all the time. When appropriate, tell the children about how people look away when they are thinking and then back at the person's eyes when they start to talk again, and that the listener looks most of the time.

6. Have the children draw pictures of different types of appropriate and inappropriate eye contact and label them as good and bad.

7. Demonstrate appropriate and inappropriate body position.

8. Write out the rules for eye contact and have the children copy them.

RULES FOR EYE CONTACT AND BODY POSITION

- STOP
- THINK (shouldn't I make eye contact and turn to the person?)
- GO!

When you are talking to someone or the person is talking to you:
- – Turn your body toward the person
- – Look at the other person's eyes
- – Look most of the time but don't stare

---

9. Demonstrate appropriate and inappropriate body proximity.

10. Have the children draw pictures of appropriate and inappropriate proximity and label them (discuss proximity with family vs. friends and acquaintances).

11. Write out the rules for personal space and have the children copy them.

RULES FOR HOW CLOSE I SHOULD GET

- STOP
- THINK (am I too close or too far away from the other person?)
- GO!
  - – Stay one arm's length away

---

12. Have the children approach you to make a request or start a conversation. Cue them with STOP and THINK ABOUT EYES AND BODY.

13. Hand out homework, including a blank graphic organizer.

Social Skills Homework #11:
Your Body Speaks – EYES, BODY POSITION, PROXIMITY

Dear Parents,

Today we learned about rules for eye contact and body position and proximity.

1. Write a Personal Story (use the graphic organizer) *with* your child about something that happens between sessions.

2. Please review the work in your child's notebook. Go over the rules and have your child demonstrate the correct and incorrect use of body position, proximity, and eye contact.

3. Watch a videotape or movie with your child. Talk about what you both see. Talk about eye contact, body position, and proximity.

4. Practice cuing your child with the words STOP AND THINK ABOUT EYES AND BODY. If possible, videotape your child interacting with you and watch the video together; evaluate for eye contact and body position. Practice in the following situations: drawing or coloring, doing homework, talking (less eye contact is appropriate during motor activities).

Child's Homework

Please answer the following questions. Write your answers on a separate sheet of paper. Do this with one of your parents. (*Parents, remember, if your child has difficulty writing the responses, you may write them in.*)

1. What is appropriate eye contact?

2. Why is it important to make appropriate eye contact?

3. What is the rule about how close you should be to others?

4. How does the other person feel if you get too close?

5. How does the person feel if you are too far away?

6. Why should you face a person when you are talking or the person is talking to you?

What happened?

_____
_____
_____
_____

My Personal Story

Consequences?

_____
_____
_____
_____

What should you do next time?

_____
_____
_____
_____

Social Skills Lesson #12

YOUR BODY SPEAKS TOO – VOICE

Goal:

To learn rules for appropriate volume and tone of voice.

Materials

- blackboard and chalk
- loose-leaf paper
- markers
- 2 containers for the index cards
- index cards with situations written on them (Step 5)
- index cards with things to say written on them (Step 5)
- copies of handouts and homework
  Social Skills Homework: *Your Body Speaks Too – Voice* (p.124)
  Graphic organizer for Personal Story (p.125)

Note: Make students put handouts and other materials in the appropriate section of their notebooks after each lesson.

1. Review homework.

2. Go over Personal Stories, discussing other options for the behavior in the situation (with older students focus on consequences of actions – how one's actions affect others and oneself).

3. Talk about the purpose of the lesson (*using appropriate voice volume*).

4. Demonstrate soft, medium, and loud voices and let the children try them out. With the youngest children, it is helpful for them to have pictures of different animals with which they can identify each volume of voice (e.g., Loud Lion, Medium Puppy, Quiet Fish). Talk about situations in which you would use each voice volume.

5. Play the volume game. You will need two containers. In container #1, put index cards with situations written on them (e.g., You are in class and your teacher is giving directions). In container #2, put index cards with statements about things to say (e.g., Tell your friend you need a pencil). Have the children pick one card from each container. Their job is to use an appropriate volume for the situation depicted.

6. Write out the rules for appropriate volume of voice and have the children copy them.

RULES FOR VOLUME OF VOICE
- STOP, THINK (what volume should I use?)
- GO!
    - Sometimes you need to speak louder than normal and sometimes more quietly
    - Make sure the person you are talking to can hear you
    - BUT do not disturb others

---

7. Demonstrate good and poor use of volume (supply the situation; e.g., on the playground vs. in the library) and ask the kids to tell you whether you were appropriate or not.

8. Hand out homework, including a blank graphic organizer.

Social Skills Homework #12:
Your Body Speaks Too-VOICE

Dear Parents,

1. Today we learned about rules for volume of voice and tone of voice.

2. Write a Personal Story (use the graphic organizer) *with* your child about something that happens between sessions.

3. Please review the work in your child's notebook. Go over all rules.

4. Point out when you, your child, or others are using different voice volume in different situations this week.

Child's Homework

Please answer the following questions. Write your answers on a separate sheet of paper. Do this with one of your parents. (*Parents, remember, if your child has difficulty writing the responses, you may write them in.*)

What volume should you use when:

1. You see your friend walking down the block?

2. Your dad is asleep?

3. You are in the kitchen with your mom, who is cooking dinner?

4. Your mom is on the phone?

5. You are at a baseball game?

Personal Story Organizer

What
happened?

_____

_____

_____

_____

**My Personal
Story**

Consequences?

_____

_____

_____

_____

What should
you do next
time?

_____

_____

_____

_____

Social Skills Lesson #13

REVIEW

Goal:

To review pull-out lessons #1-12.

Materials

- social skills notebooks
- social skills test #1 (page 127)

1. Review homework.

2. Go over Personal Stories, discussing other options for behavior in the situation (with older students focus on consequences of actions – how one's actions affect others and oneself).

3. Talk about the purpose of the lesson *(review all social skills lessons to date and give test)*.

4. Ask all children the questions on the test.
   Give the written test to older children for homework. Have the other students complete the test in class.

Lesson #13
Social Skills Test #1

Name:_____

1. What are the three steps for stopping an inappropriate behavior like acting too silly or too angry?

    1.

    2.

    3.

2. Tell how to interrupt someone appropriately. Tell about a situation when you would *not* interrupt someone.

    1.

    2.

    3.

3. How should you greet your friends when you see them at school? What should your eyes be doing? What kind of expression should you have on your face?

4. If you don't know what to do or you are having trouble with something in class, how do you ask your teacher for help?

5. Write a compliment.

6. What are three things you can do to be a good friend?

    1.

    2.

    3.

7. How far away from a person should you be when you are talking to him or playing with him?

8. Why is it important to take responsibility for your own things, your own homework, etc.? Why is it important to be responsible for helping other people?

9. What do you want other people to think about you? (Do you want them to think you are nice, smart, good at sports, respectful, thoughtful, responsible, etc.?) Why?

Social Skills Lesson #14

LISTENING SKILLS

Goal:

To learn the rules for listening.

Materials

- blackboard and chalk
- loose-leaf paper
- markers
- sheet of butcher paper (large enough to trace a child's body outline on)
- tape
- copies of handouts and homework
  Handout A, *Listening* (p.131)
  Social Skills Homework: *Listening Skills* (p.132)
  Graphic organizer for Personal Story (p.133)

Note: Make sure students put handouts and other materials in the appropriate section of their notebooks after each lesson.

1. Review homework.

2. Go over Personal Stories, discussing other options for behavior in the situation (with older students focus on consequences of actions – how one's actions affect others and oneself).

3. Talk about the purpose of the lesson (*understanding how to listen*).

4. Have the children sit quietly for 2 minutes and just listen. Tell them to remember what they hear. Then have them write (or you may write on the board) a list of the things they heard. Ask them what their ears and mouths were doing while they listened.

5. Choose a volunteer to be traced onto the piece of butcher paper. Let all the children help to trace the child. Tape the "person" onto the wall. Now draw eyes, ears, nose, and mouth. With an arrow pointing to each part of the body, write what a given part should be doing while a person is listening. (Eyes look at the person who is talking; mouth is quiet; head nods; body faces the person; brain is thinking about what the person is saying.) Tell them the listener's and the speaker's brains MUST think about the *same* thing. It is not enough for the listener to simply sit quietly and look.

6. Write out the rules for appropriate listening and have the children copy.

RULES FOR LISTENING
- STOP
- THINK (what should my body and brain be doing while I listen?)
- GO!
  - Eyes look
  - Body faces person
  - Head nods
  - Ears hear what is being said
  - Brain thinks about what person is talking about
  - Mouth is quiet or says, "Uh huh"

---

7. Give the students copies of Handout A to put in their notebooks.

8. Demonstrate appropriate and inappropriate listening and ask the children to tell you whether you were appropriate or not.

9. Talk about the fact that we need to listen much more than we talk. Have the children draw pie graphs that show approximately the amount someone should talk relative to how much he or she should listen given the number of people in the conversation. For example, if there are three people in the group, each person should talk 1/3 of the time. For a group of five, each person talks approximately 1/5 of the time. The pie charts are intended to make the point the child should talk less and listen more.

10. Play a special game of "stop and go" called "Stop When I Speak," where the children jump or move and stop when the leader begins to speak. When the leader speaks, they not only stop all activity, they also face the speaker, look at the speaker, and put a finger to their lips.

11. Hand out homework, including a blank graphic organizer.

Social Skills Homework #14:
Listening Skills

Dear Parents,

Today we learned about rules for what your body should be doing when you are listening.

1. Write a Personal Story (use the graphic organizer) *with* your child about something that happens between sessions.

2. Please review the work in your child's notebook. Go over all rules.

3. Help your child practice listening skills this week.

4. Play a special game of "stop and go" called "Stop When I Speak," where you have your child jump or move and stop when you begin to speak. When you speak, your child should not only stop all activity, but also face you, look at you, and put a finger to his or her lips.

Child's Homework

Please answer the following questions. Write your answers on a separate sheet of paper. Do this with one of your parents. (*Parents, remember, if your child has difficulty writing the responses, you may write them in.*)

1. What should your brain be doing when you are listening?

2. What should your eyes be doing when you are listening?

3. What position should your body be in when you are listening?

4. What should your mouth be doing when you are listening?

What
happened?

_____
_____
_____
_____

**My Personal
Story**

Consequences?

_____
_____
_____
_____

What should
you do next
time?

_____
_____
_____

Social Skills Lesson #15
CONVERSATIONS: PART 2 – SMALL TALK

Goal:

To learn the "two-question rule" for small talk.

Materials

- blackboard and chalk
- loose-leaf paper
- markers
- conversation strip from Lesson #4 (pp. 85-88)
- copies of handouts and homework
  Handout A, *Four Parts of a Conversation* (p.136)
  Handout B, *Some Questions to Start Small Talk* (p.137)
  Social Skills Homework: *"Two-Question Rule"* and *Small Talk* (pp. 138-139)
  Graphic organizer for Personal Story (p.140)

Note: Make sure students put handouts and other materials in the appropriate section of their notebooks each lesson.

1. Review homework.

2. Go over Personal Stories, discussing other options for behavior in the situation (with older students focus on consequences of actions – how one's actions affect others and oneself).

3. Talk about the purpose of the lesson (*knowing what to do after initiating an interaction – specifically how to respond to a question*).

4. Review the four parts of a conversation while showing the children the conversation strip. Give children Handout A, *Four Parts of a Conversation*.

5. Write out the "two-question rule" and have the children copy.

"TWO-QUESTION RULE"
- STOP, THINK (I hear a question; what question can I ask?)
- GO!
  - When someone asks a question, answer it
  - Then ask a similar question
  - Wait for a response
  - TAKE TURNS

---

6. Have the children line up and one at a time try using the "two-question rule" with you. Ask each child, "How are you?" The child should answer and then ask the same question, "How are you?" and wait for a response.

7. Distribute Handout B, *Some Questions to Start Small Talk*, to start small talk, including questions about classes, recess, and television.

8. Ask each child a different question and have him/her respond according to the "two-question rule." Then give children an opportunity to practice the rule with each other.

9. Practice the "stop and go" game with the children, having them stop whenever the leader talks.

10. Hand out homework, including a blank graphic organizer.

The "two-question" rule is from *Social Skills Training for Children and Adolescents with Asperger Syndrome and Social-Communication Problems* by J. Baker (Shawnee Mission, KS: Asperger and Autism Publishing Company, 2003), p. 92. Reprinted with permission.

Greeting: "Hello"

Small Talk: (Make sure it is appropriate to have small talk. Do not initiate small talk if the person you are talking with is very busy. Go straight to the main topic.)

Main topic: Make a point/listen for the point/ stay on topic

Continue:
- Ask questions
- Make comments
- Add information

Closing: "Good-bye"

Handout B, Lesson #15
Some Questions to Start Small Talk

1. How are you?

2. How was your day?

3. Did you have a nice weekend?

4. What are you going to do this weekend?

5. What did you think of (the test, math, the ballgame last night, etc.)?

6. Did you see anything good on TV last night?

7. What do you want to do during recess today?

Social Skills Homework #15:
Conversations: Part 2–Small Talk

Dear Parents,

Today we learned about the "two-question rule." (When someone asks a question, answer it. Then ask a similar question.)

1. Write a Personal Story (use the graphic organizer) *with* your child about something that happens between sessions.

2. Please review the work in your child's notebook. Go over all rules.

3. Practice with your child. Ask a question and have your child respond by answering the question and then asking a similar question.

Child's Homework

1. Use the picture of the children with the conversation bubbles in your notebook. In the conversation bubble above each child's head, write a statement and a question in one bubble. In the other bubble, write a response to the question followed by a similar question.

Social Skills Homework #15:
SMALL TALK

What happened?

_____
_____
_____
_____

My Personal Story

Consequences?

_____
_____
_____
_____

What should you do next time?

_____
_____
_____
_____

Social Skills Lesson #16
INDOOR RECESS SURVIVAL

Goal:

To learn and practice age-appropriate games and activities for indoor recess.

Materials

- blackboard and chalk
- loose-leaf paper
- markers
- a deck of cards
- board games
- copies of handouts and homework
  Social Skills Homework: *Indoor Recess Survival* (p.143)
  Graphic organizer for Personal Story (p.144)

Note: Make sure students put handouts and other materials in the appropriate section of their notebooks after each lesson.

1. Review homework.

2. Go over Personal Stories, discussing other options for behavior in the situation (with older students focus on the consequences of actions – include a discussion of how one's actions affect others and oneself).

3. Talk about the purpose of the lesson (*learning what to do during indoor recess*).

4. Throughout this lesson, emphasize that peer mentors will be there to help the children during indoor recess.

5. Make a list with the children of the kinds of games and activities they see the other children play; have each child write the list in his/her notebook.

6. Teach the children the rules for various games and give them the opportunity to practice with each other. Choose games from the list generated by the children or games such as board games that are readily available, card games like "war," "go fish," etc. Indoor gym games may be taught as well. Teach and play at least two games, and have the children practice approaching another child to ask him or her to play.

7. Line the children up and practice greetings and the "two-question rule" for small talk with each, one at a time.

8. Hand out homework, including a blank graphic organizer. Have the children write two games on the homework sheet to be practiced at home. These should be games that you have observed the children's peers play during recess or that the peer mentors have mentioned.

Social Skills Homework #16:
Indoor Recess Survival

Dear Parents,

Today we reviewed and learned rules for a variety of games that may be played in indoor recess.

1. Write a Personal Story (use the graphic organizer) *with* your child about something that happens between sessions.

2. Make a list of simple chores that your child could do on a daily basis and that he/she does not do already. Send the list to school in your child's social skills notebook. We need this list so that we can assign your child a "secret responsibility" to do at home. You will not know which chore is chosen, but the idea is that your child will carry it out well enough on a daily basis so that you will be able to guess what the responsibility was by the end of the week.

3. Please review the work in your child's notebook.

4. If possible, send a deck of cards with your child to indoor recess. This will give your child the opportunity to approach other children and ask them to play a structured game.

5. Your child's peers play a number of games regularly during recess. Two of these games are listed below. Please practice playing the following games with your child:

1. _____

2. _____

Personal Story Organizer

What happened?

_____
_____
_____
_____
_____

My Personal Story

Consequences?

_____
_____
_____
_____
_____

What should you do next time?

_____
_____
_____
_____

Social Skills Lesson #17

I HAVE THE POWER #1: RESPONSIBILITY

Goals:

Teach the children to take responsibility for their personal belongings and behavior.

Materials

- blackboard and chalk
- loose-leaf paper
- markers
- pencils
- crayons
- copies of handouts and homework
  Handout A, *Rules for Responsibility* (p.147)
  Social Skills Homework: *I Have the Power #1: Responsibility* (p.148)
  Graphic organizer for Personal Story (p.149)

Note: Make sure students put handouts and other materials in the appropriate section of their notebooks after each lesson.

1. Review homework.

2. Go over Personal Stories, discussing other options for behavior in the situation (with older students focus on consequences of actions – how one's actions affect others and oneself).

3. As the children come to the classroom door, tell them that each of them will have a secret responsibility. Whisper to them what their responsibility is. Each child is to carry out the responsibility in front of the other children, who are to watch carefully and guess what a given child's responsibility is. The responsibilities are: pass out a sheet of paper to each child, pass out a pencil to each child, pass out crayons, etc. That way, all children will have the materials to do a drawing according to teacher instructions. Ask the children to identify the job that each child had.

4. Have the children do a drawing.

5. Now collect all of the materials. Then take the kids out of the room and repeat Step 3, but this time tell one child to fail to meet his or her responsibility. (Tell him what his job is but that you want to see what happens if he does not do it. Tell him not to do his job – e.g., handing out paper, but no pencils.) As a result, it will not be possible to complete the drawing. Discuss how

people depend on each other to be responsible for their own jobs and that things do not work well if someone fails to live up to his or her responsibility. Also, talk about how the other kids feel about a person who is not responsible.

6. Make a list of school responsibilities and a list of home responsibilities. Make sure to include the responsibilities of following school rules and keeping control of one's reactions to strong feelings.

7. Talk about the purpose of the lesson (*understanding who and what the children control and are responsible for and who controls them*); explain that the children control whether they do or don't do the right thing.

8. Distribute Handout A, *Rules for Responsibility,* and discuss.

RULES FOR RESPONSIBILITY
- STOP, THINK (what is the responsible thing to do?)
- GO!
    - I HAVE THE POWER to control ME
    - I **do not** control others
    - Other people (my parents and teachers) are my helpers; they tell me the rules
    - I need to make good choices to do the right things according to the rules
    - If I do the right thing, people will feel good about me and like me

---

9. Demonstrate I HAVE THE POWER in the following situations and ask the children whether you are being responsible (kids can try the situations too):
    - frustration with homework – doing it and asking for help when needed vs. trying to force your mother to do it for you
    - anger that someone does not want to play the game you want to play – screaming or twisting their arm vs. controlling self and suggesting turns or just playing the other child's game

10. Help each child to come up with a personal goal. (It should be one of the child's behaviors that he or she wants to take responsibility for and control of.) Have the children write the goal in their social skills notebook.

11. Hand out homework, including a blank graphic organizer.

12. Choose a secret responsibility for each child (see p. 148).

RULES FOR RESPONSIBILITY

- I HAVE THE POWER to control ME.

- I **do not** control others.

- Parents and teachers are my helpers; they tell me the rules.

- I need to make good choices to do the right things according to the rules.

- If I do the right thing, people will feel good about me and like me.

Social Skills Homework #17:
I Have the Power #1: Responsibility

Dear Parents,

Today we learned about rules about responsibility and being in control of oneself, not others.

1. Write a Personal Story (use the graphic organizer) *with* your child about something that happens between sessions.

2. Please review the work in your child's notebook. Go over all rules.

3. Your child has a secret responsibility at home this week. The child is supposed to carry out this responsibility so well that by the end of the week you can guess what it is. Please send your guess in a note in the social skills notebook (communication section). Do not ask your child what the responsibility is. Let the child feel that the responsibility is totally his/hers.

Child's Homework

Please answer the following questions. Write your answers on a separate sheet of paper. Do this with one of your parents. (*Parents, remember, if your child has difficulty writing the responses, you may write them in.*)

1. Do your secret responsibility at home.

2. Answer the following questions:

   - Who do you have the power to control?

   - Can you control others?

   - What should you do if you are upset by what someone else is doing?

Personal Story Organizer

What happened?

_____
_____
_____
_____

My Personal Story

Consequences?

_____
_____
_____
_____

What should you do next time?

_____
_____
_____
_____

Social Skills Lesson #18

DEALING WITH ANGER

Goals:
To help children develop strategies for coping with angry feelings.

Materials

- blackboard and chalk
- loose-leaf paper
- markers
- book: *Let's Talk About Feeling Angry*, J. Berry (Scholastic Inc., 1995) or *Mad Isn't Bad: A Child's Book about Anger*, M. Mundy (Abbey Press, 1999)
- copies of handouts and homework
  Handout A, *Graphic Organizer: Anger* (p. 154)
  Handout B, *Rules for Dealing with Anger* (p. 156)
  Social Skills Homework: *Dealing with Anger* (p. 157)
  Graphic organizer for Personal Story (p. 158)

Note: Make sure students put handouts and other materials in the appropriate section of their notebooks after each lesson.

1. Review homework.

2. Go over Personal Stories, discussing other options for behavior in the situation (with older students focus on consequences of actions – how one's actions affect others and oneself).

3. Talk about the purpose of the lesson (*understanding how to deal with angry feelings*).

4. Read "Jimmy Gets Too Angry" (p. 152) while showing the children the cartoon strip (p.153). (You may also act out the story to make the point clearer.) Emphasize that it is most important to be able to stop angry behavior so that it is possible to think of the appropriate thing to do; talk about the consequences for Jimmy when he did not stop.

5. Read the book *Let's Talk About Feeling Angry* or *Mad Isn't Bad* to the children.

6. Read the book again, but this time stop and identify each subtopic (i.e., things that make you angry, how you feel, what you do, what you don't do). Have the children fill in the topic (feeling angry), subtopics and details on the graphic organizer (Handout A) that includes main topic and

subtopics from the book. Have them add personal details about things that make them angry and what they should do and not do in addition to the things mentioned in the book. With older children, discuss when it might not be appropriate to talk to the person one feels angry with (e.g., when one's rights are violated, if this would endanger the child of possibly being threatened).

7. Give the children copies of Handout B, *Rules for Dealing with Anger.*

8. Hand out homework, including a blank graphic organizer.

9. Choose a secret responsibility for each child.

"Jimmy Gets Too Angry"

One day in gym class the kids were playing soccer. Jimmy loved to play soccer, but he hated to lose. The game was almost over. Billy was on Jimmy's team. Billy kicked the ball hard to try to make a goal to win the game, but he missed. Jimmy got really angry. First he screamed at Billy, then he hit him. The teacher sent Jimmy to the principal's office and called his parents to tell them what happened.

Jimmy Gets Too Angry

Handout A, Lesson #18:
Description Organizer: Anger

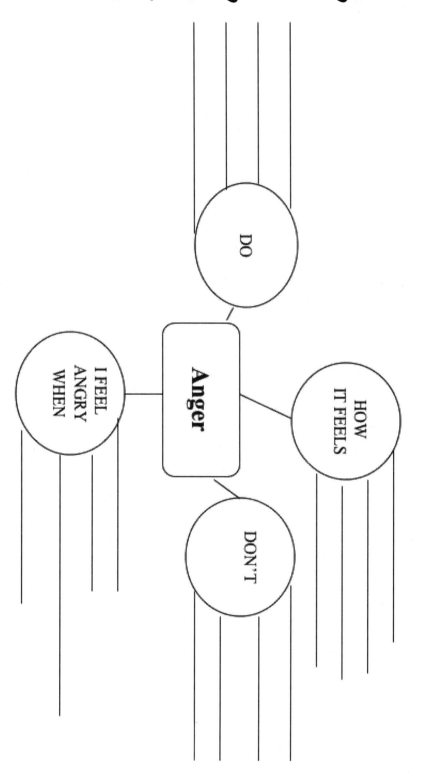

Handout A, Lesson #18:
Sample Description Organizer: Anger

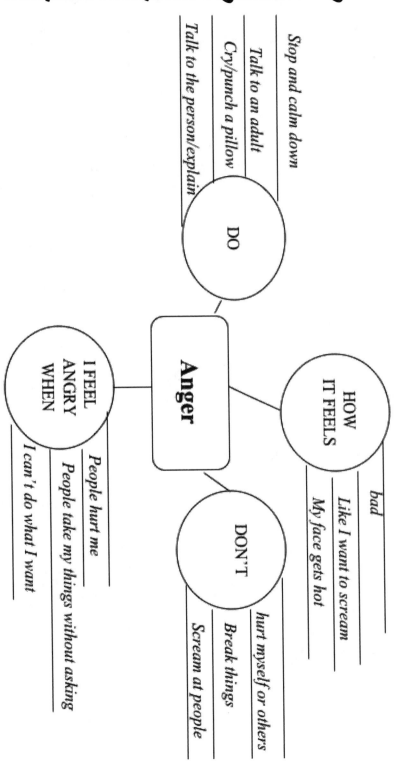

RULES FOR DEALING WITH ANGER

STOP,

THINK (What should and what shouldn't I do when I am angry?)

DO	**DON'T**
STOP	Hurt others
Calm down (walk away for a time if you need to)	Hurt yourself
Talk to an adult about how you feel (say "I feel angry because …")	Scream
	Break things
Talk to the person you are angry with (say "I feel angry because …") if this is appropriate	Try to control everyone else
Be fair	

Social Skills Homework #18:
Dealing with Anger

Dear Parents,

Today we learned about rules for dealing with anger.

1. Write a Personal Story (use the graphic organizer) *with* your child about something that happens between sessions.

2. Please review the work in your child's notebook. Go over all rules.

3. Your child has a secret responsibility at home this week. The child is supposed to carry out this responsibility so well that by the end of the week you can guess what it is. Please send your guess in a note in the social skills notebook. Do not ask your child what the responsibility is. Let him/her feel that he/she is totally responsible.

Child's Homework

1. Do your secret responsibility.

2. Talk to two people about what makes you angry and what you should do when you are angry. Use the graphic organizer that we made in class to help you talk about these things.

Personal Story Organizer

What happened?

_____
_____
_____
_____

My Personal Story

Consequences?

_____
_____
_____
_____

What should you do next time?

_____
_____
_____
_____

Social Skills Lesson #19

I HAVE THE POWER #2: MISTAKES AND APOLOGIZING

Goals:

To discuss what people should do if they make a mistake.

Materials

- blackboard and chalk
- loose-leaf paper
- markers
- index cards
- a hat
- copies of handouts and homework
  Handout A, *Examples of Mistakes Children Make* (p.161)
  Social Skills Homework: *Mistakes and Apologizing* (p.162)
  Graphic organizer for Personal Story (p.163)

Note: Make sure students put handouts and other materials in the appropriate section of their notebooks after each lesson.

1. Review homework.

2. Go over Personal Stories, discussing other options for behavior in the situation (with older students focus on consequences of actions – how one's actions affect others and oneself).

3. Talk about the purpose of the lesson (*understanding what to do if I make a mistake*). Emphasize that everyone makes mistakes and may be forgiven and that people can stop in the middle of making a mistake.

4. Distribute Handout A and talk about the kinds of mistakes that kids can make. Tailor this discussion to your group of students. Examples of mistakes include: hurting self or others (physically or by being mean), screaming at others, getting too silly, being a sore loser, failing to follow social skills rules. Have each child write down a mistake that that he/she tends to make and will work to correct in the future.

5. Write out the rules concerning what to do about mistakes and have the children copy them.

RULES ABOUT MISTAKES
- STOP (remind the kids that this is the hardest time to stop)
- THINK ("what should I do when I make a mistake?")
  - I can stop in the middle of making a mistake or losing control
  - I can apologize in the middle of a mistake ("Oops, I lost my head") or after I have made a mistake
  - I can say what I am sorry for ("I'm sorry for_____")
  - I can say what I will do differently next time. ("Next time I will _____")
- GO!
  - Keep stopping
  - Apologize

---

6. Write mistakes people can make on index cards and put them into a hat. Have the children take turns selecting a card from the hat. The child role-plays the mistake depicted on the card. Have the children practice the Rules About Mistakes.

7. Hand out homework, including a blank graphic organizer.

8. Choose a secret responsibility for each child.

Handout A, Lesson #19:
Examples of Mistakes Children Make

Barbara Wygoda and Susan Levine

1. You bump into someone.

2. You speak in a loud voice during silent reading and disturb your classmates.

3. You did the wrong page in your spelling workbook for homework.

4. Your pencil is missing and you start yelling at the kid sitting next to you.

5. You make a mean face at your friend.

6. You call your brother "stupid" when you are angry with him.

7. Your friend is reading a book that you want to see, so you grab it from him.

8. You call out an answer in class without raising your hand.

9. You know your mom hates it when you kick or throw stones around in the park. You start to do it anyway.

Social Skills Homework #19:
I Have the Power #2: Mistakes and Apologizing

Dear Parents,

Today we learned about rules for what to do if you start making a mistake or begin losing control. The most important things the children learned are that everyone makes mistakes and that they can stop in the middle of making a mistake.

1. Write a Personal Story (use the graphic organizer) *with* your child about something that happens between sessions.

2. Please review the work in your child's notebook. Go over all rules.

3. Your child has a secret responsibility at home this week. The child is supposed to carry out this responsibility so well that by the end of the week you can guess what it is. Please send your guess in a note in the social skills notebook. Do not ask your child what the responsibility is. Let him/her feel that he/she is totally responsible.

Child's Homework

Please answer the following questions. Write your answers on a separate sheet of paper. Do this with one of your parents. (*Parents, remember, if your child has difficulty writing the responses, you may write them in.*)

1. Do your secret responsibility.

2. Answer the following questions:

- What should you do if you start to lose control?

- What can you do if you are in the middle of making a mistake?

- What is the important rule about mistakes?

Personal Story Organizer

What happened?

_____
_____
_____
_____

My Personal Story

Consequences?

_____
_____
_____
_____

What should you do next time?

_____
_____
_____
_____

Social Skills Lesson #20

CONVERSATIONS: PART 3 – THE MAIN POINT (TALKING ON A TOPIC)

Goals:

To learn the rules for initiating and talking about a topic. To learn to generate a topic sentence.

Materials

- blackboard and chalk
- loose-leaf paper
- markers
- empty shoebox
- slips of paper with topics written on them (p. 167)
- copies of handouts and homework
  Handout A, *Sample Event Organizer* (p. 166)
  Social Skills Homework: *Conversations: Part 3 – The Main Point* (p.168)
  Graphic organizer for Personal Story (p.169)

Note: Make sure students put handouts and other materials in the appropriate section of their notebooks after each lesson.

1. Review homework.

2. Go over Personal Stories, discussing other options for behavior in the situation (with older students focus on consequences of actions – how one's actions affect others and oneself).

3. Talk about the purpose of the lesson (*learning how to start and talk on a topic*).

4. Make a graphic organizer on the board about an event – school trip, an assembly, a holiday, or what a particular child in the group did over the weekend (p. 166). Have the children copy the graphic organizer onto a piece of paper. Talk about and identify the main topic and subtopics. Show the children how to make a topic sentence about the main topic and each subtopic. Have them try making topic sentences on their own. Number the main topic #1; number the subtopics in the order in which they will be discussed. Model how to use the graphic organizer. First generate a topic sentence about the main topic. Then give a topic sentence about a subtopic, followed by all of the details. Go on to talk about each of the other subtopics in the same way. Give a concluding sentence. Then let each child try.

5. Write out the rules for talking about a topic and have the children copy them.

RULES FOR TALKING ABOUT TOPICS
- STOP
- THINK
  - What will I say?
  - I will talk about a main topic and then subtopics
- GO!
  - Start with a topic sentence about the main topic
  - Use a topic sentence for your first subtopic
  - Tell the details about your first subtopic
  - Talk about your other subtopics; always start with a topic sentence

---

6. Write topics on slips of paper (see p. 167) and put them in the shoebox. Have each child draw a slip out of the box. Their job is to make a topic sentence about the topic they draw. Topics might include: my weekend; what I like to play on the playground; baseball; my favorite book; favorite movie; my pet.

7. Hand out homework, including a blank graphic organizer.

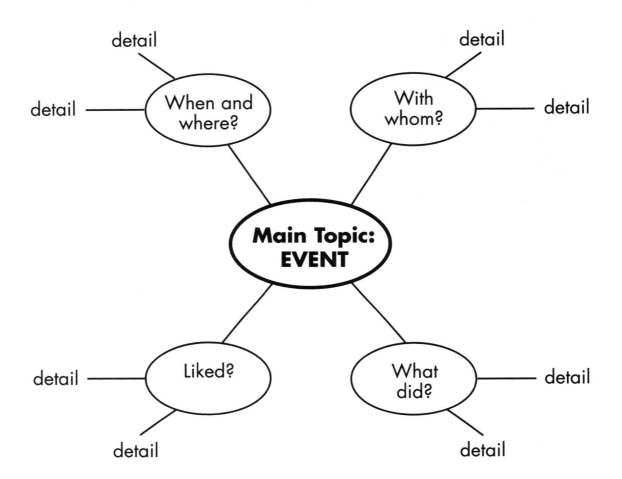

Examples of Topics for #6

Grandparents

My mom

My pet

A holiday

Summer vacation

Baseball

Going to the park

Eating in a restaurant

Weather

Music

The rainforest

The president

Frogs

Social Skills Homework #20:
Conversations: Part 3 – The Main Point (Talking on a Topic)

Dear Parents,

Today we learned about rules for starting a topic and talking about it.

1. Write a Personal Story (use the graphic organizer) *with* your child about something that happens between sessions.

2. Please review the work in your child's notebook. Go over all rules.

3. Help your child with his/her graphic organizer and help him/her practice talking from the graphic organizer. A sample of the graphic organizer is included with this homework.

Child's Homework

Draw a graphic organizer about your favorite vacation. The main topic is the vacation. The subtopics are *with whom? where and when? what did? liked?* Fill in the details.

Personal Story Organizer

What happened?

_____

_____

_____

_____

My Personal Story

Consequences?

_____

_____

_____

_____

What should you do next time?

_____

_____

_____

_____

Social Skills Lesson #21:

CONVERSATIONS: PART 3 – MAIN POINT (RECOGNIZING TOPICS)

PLEASE NOTE: THIS LESSON MAY BE REPEATED OR SPLIT INTO TWO LESSONS – ONE DEALING WITH THE MAIN TOPIC OF LANGUAGE, THE OTHER DEALING WITH THE MAIN TOPIC OF PLAY OR ANOTHER OBSERVED ACTIVITY.

Goals:

To learn how to determine the main topic of language and play.

Materials

- blackboard and chalk
- loose-leaf paper
- markers
- copies of handouts and homework
  Social Skills Homework: *Conversations: Part 3 – Recognizing Topics* (p.173)
  Graphic organizers for Personal Stories (p.174)

Note: Make sure students put handouts and other materials in the appropriate section of their notebooks after each lesson.

1. Review homework. (Look at the children's graphic organizers about their vacation. Make sure they are completed correctly. If not, help them correct them. Collect them and keep for use at the next session.)

2. Go over Personal Stories, discussing other options for behavior in the situation (with older students focus on consequences of actions – how one's actions affect others and oneself).

3. Talk about the purpose of the lesson (*figuring out the main topic*).

4. Play "Name That Category." Read lists of items belonging to a category (p. 172) and ask the children to label the category. Note that some groups of items belong to superordinate categories; others require labeling novel categories.

5. Read a couple of short factual passages (from books about animals or from a science or social studies textbook). Have the children decide what the topic of the passage is as they are listen-

ing. Ask what the topic is. If this is difficult for the children, list details from the passage on the board and ask the children to name the category to which they belong.

6. Choose a child from the group and play a game with him/her (e.g., board game, catch). Ask the other children in the group what the topic of the play is.

7. Write out the rules for the first thing to do when you are in a new situation and have the children copy them.

RULES ABOUT WHAT TO DO FIRST IN A NEW SITUATION
- STOP
- THINK (What should I do first?)
  - Find the main topic
  - Is it a good time to start playing or talking with the others?
  - If YES,
- GO!
  - Play or talk about the same topic as the other people
  - Stick to the topic

---

8. Stage a conversation with another adult or one of the children in the group. Have the other children identify your topic.

9. Have the children play activities and/or read from a book. Demonstrate how to inappropriately go off topic (e.g., comments like "You know what I had for dinner last night?"). Have the children tell you what you should have done.

10. Hand out homework, including a blank graphic organizer.

"NAME THAT CATEGORY"

1. dog, cat, frog, fish

2. airplane, bus, car, bicycle

3. yellow, sings sweetly, flies, cage

4. flour, yeast, dough, oven

5. ice cream, roller coaster, cotton candy, ferris wheel

6. dolphin, blow hole, 7 minutes under water, lungs

These sets of words may be written on cards or on the blackboard. Pictures may also be drawn to accompany the words.

Social Skills Homework #21:
Conversations: Part 3 – Recognizing Topics

Dear Parents,

Today we learned about recognizing the main topic of language and play.

1. Write a Personal Story (use the graphic organizer) *with* your child about something that happens between sessions.

2. Please review the work in your child's notebook. Go over all rules.

3. Read your child simple factual material about an animal, place, etc., and ask him/her to identify the main topic. After you read each paragraph, ask your child to identify the subtopic in the paragraph.

4. Ask your child to listen to a short conversation you have with another adult. Ask your child to identify the topic.

5. Watch some children at play and ask your child to identify the topic of the play.

What
happened?

_____
_____
_____
_____
_____

My Personal Story

Consequences?

_____
_____
_____
_____

What should
you do next
time?

_____
_____
_____
_____

Social Skills Lesson #22

CONVERSATIONS: PART 3 – MAIN TOPIC (TALKING FROM GRAPHIC ORGANIZER AND CONTINUING THE TOPIC WITH QUESTIONS)

Goals:

To learn the rules for continuing the main topic of a conversation.

Materials

- blackboard and chalk
- loose-leaf paper
- markers
- copies of handouts and homework
  Social Skills Homework: *Conversations: Part 3 – Continuing the Topic with Questions* (p.178)
  Graphic organizer for Personal Story (p.179)

Note: Make sure students put handouts and other materials in the appropriate section of their notebooks after each lesson.

1. Go over Personal Stories, discussing other options for behavior in the situation (with older students focus on consequences of actions – how one's actions affect others and oneself).

2. Talk about the purpose of the lesson (*identifying the topic of a conversation and continuing by asking questions*).

3. Play "What Is the Topic?" Talk to the children about a topic (e.g., an animal) and then ask them to name the topic. Do this with two other topics (e.g., your weekend or a holiday, an upcoming event).

4. Read the story on page 177 to the students. Read it again. On the second reading, after you read the first sentence, stop and ask the children what the topic is (in the topic sentence). Point out that the person who wrote the story does not stick to the topic! Ask the children to listen to the rest of the story and to tell you every time the topic shifts. (For older children, have them label each topic as well when the topic shifts.)

5. Write out the rules for appropriate topic maintenance in conversation and have the children copy them.

```
┌─────────────────────────────────────────────────────────────────┐
│  RULES FOR CONTINUING ON A TOPIC IN CONVERSATION – #1             │
│    •  STOP                                                         │
│    •  THINK (what is the topic?)                                   │
│    •  GO!                                                          │
│       –  Stick to the topic                                        │
│       –  Ask questions                                             │
└─────────────────────────────────────────────────────────────────┘
```

6. Tell the children they will be practicing how to continue a conversation by asking questions. Have them use the graphic organizers that they generated about vacations (p. 166). Select one child to talk through his/her graphic organizer. (Help the children generate a topic sentence for the main topic and each subtopic on their graphic organizer.) Then point to each of the other children in the group in turn and ask them to ask a question. Write the following words on the blackboard to help the students generate questions: *who, what, when, where, why, how.* If the children cannot think of what to ask, prompt them by whispering a question for them to use. (If you are working with an individual child, take turns with the child, talking about vacations and asking questions.)

7. Hand out homework, including a blank graphic organizer.

Story for Lesson #22

I love to go to the zoo. It is fun to see all of the animals there. My favorite animals are the gorillas. My brother's favorite animals are the giraffes. My brother is in kindergarten. He loves school. In school he is learning to write his name. He also plays and listens to stories. My favorite story is *The Three Bears*. I really like the part when the bears come home and find out that someone ate all of Baby Bear's breakfast. Last night we ate pizza for dinner.

Social Skills Homework #22:
Conversations: Part 3 – Continuing the Topic with Questions

Dear Parents,

Today we learned about rules for maintaining a topic in conversation.

1. Write a Personal Story (use the graphic organizer) *with* your child about something that happens between sessions.

2. Please review the work in your child's notebook. Go over all rules.

3. Make a graphic organizer about an event in your child's life. For example, a graphic organizer might be made about a trip to the zoo, with subtopics, who, what, when, and where. Then have a conversation about the event. Your child should talk from the graphic organizer. Ask questions. (It is helpful if you identify what you are doing when you ask a question, make a comment or add information; for example, What did you like best when we went on that trip to Chicago last summer? – *I am asking a question*.)

4. Now talk about something that happened in your life. Talk to your child about a topic of interest to you. Clearly mark your topic with a topic sentence. Ask your child to identify the topic. Your child should practice *sticking to the topic by asking questions*. Prompt the child as much as necessary to stick to the topic. If necessary, you can ask another adult to talk about a topic of interest and you can prompt the questions.

Child's Homework

Please answer the following questions. Write your answers on a separate sheet of paper. Do this with one of your parents. (*Parents, remember, if your child has difficulty writing the responses, you may write them in.*)

1. Listen to a conversation at the dinner table and ask some questions. Make sure your questions are on the topic.

2. Write down two topics you talked about and the questions you asked.
    THE MORE YOU PRACTICE THESE ACTIVITIES, THE EASIER CONVERSATIONS WILL BECOME!

Personal Story Organizer

What happened?

_____
_____
_____
_____

My Personal Story

Consequences?

_____
_____
_____
_____

What should you do next time?

_____
_____
_____
_____

Social Skills Lesson #23

CONVERSATIONS: PART 3 – MAIN TOPIC (TALKING FROM GRAPHIC ORGANIZERS AND CONTINUING THE TOPIC BY MAKING COMMENTS AND ADDING INFORMATION)

Goals:

To practice making comments and adding information to continue the main topic of a conversation.

Materials

- blackboard and chalk
- loose-leaf paper
- slips of paper
- markers
- small box
- copies of handouts and homework
  Social Skills Homework: *Conversations: Part 3 – Continuing the Topic with Comments and by Adding Information* (p. 182)
  Graphic organizer for Personal Story (p. 183)

Note: Make sure students put handouts and other materials in the appropriate section of their notebooks after each lesson.

1. Go over Personal Stories, discussing other options for behavior in the situation (with older students focus on consequences of actions – how one's actions affect others and oneself).

2. Talk about the purpose of the lesson (*identifying the topic of a conversation and continuing by adding information and making comments on the topic*).

3. Review the rules for appropriate topic maintenance in conversation given during the last session. Have the children write in the additional ways for continuing a conversation (make comments and add information). Then have them chant all of the rules for continuing.

```
┌─────────────────────────────────────────────────────────────────┐
│  RULES FOR CONTINUING ON A TOPIC IN CONVERSATION – #2             │
│    •  STOP                                                        │
│    •  THINK (what is the topic?)                                  │
│    •  GO!                                                         │
│         –  Stick to the topic                                    │
│         –  Ask questions                                          │
│         –  Make comments                                         │
│         –  Add information                                       │
└─────────────────────────────────────────────────────────────────┘
```

4. To practice asking questions on a topic, write topics on slips of paper and put them in a box. Let each child select a topic from the box without looking. The child is to generate a topic sentence based on the topic selected and two details. Ask the rest of the group to label the topic. After the topic is labeled, give each child a chance to ask a question about the topic.

5. Teach the children how to make comments and add information to a topic under discussion. Have the children use the graphic organizers they generated in Lesson #20 to talk about a special event (p. 166). Select one child to talk through her graphic organizer. (Make sure the child generates a topic sentence for the main topic and each subtopic on her graphic organizer.) With the first child, demonstrate how to make a comment and how to add information. Then point to each of the other children in the group in turn and ask them to make a comment or add information. Prompt as needed. (If you are working with just one child, take turns talking about vacations and asking questions, commenting, and adding information.)

6. Hand out homework, including a blank graphic organizer.

Social Skills Homework #23:
Conversations: Part 3 – Continuing the Topic with Comments and by Adding Information

Dear Parents,

Today we learned about rules for maintaining a topic in conversation.

1. Write a Personal Story (use the graphic organizer) *with* your child about something that happens between sessions.

2. Please review the work in your child's notebook. Go over all rules.

3. Make a graphic organizer about a new event in the child's life and have a conversation about the event. Add information, and make comments. (It would be helpful if you identify what you are doing; for example, "It sounds like you had a really great time." – *I am making a comment.*)

4. Talk about something that happened in your life. Talk to your child about a topic of interest to you. Clearly mark your topic with a topic sentence. Ask your child to identify the topic. Your child should practice sticking to the topic by *making comments and adding information.* Prompt your child as much as is needed to stick to the topic. You can also ask another adult to talk about a topic of interest and you can prompt your child with comments he can make and information he can add.

Child's Homework

1. Listen to a conversation at the dinner table and *make some comments and add information.* Make sure you are on the topic.

2. Write down two topics you talked about and what you said.

_____

_____

_____

_____

Personal Story Organizer

What happened?

_____
_____
_____
_____

My Personal Story

Consequences?

_____
_____
_____
_____

What should you do next time?

_____
_____
_____
_____

Social Skills Lesson #24

CONVERSATIONS: PRACTICING THE PARTS

Goals:

To practice the parts of a conversation.

Materials

- blackboard and chalk
- loose-leaf paper
- markers
- long sheet of paper (to draw a large cartoon strip of the parts of a conversation)
- tape
- copies of handouts and homework
  Social Skills Homework: *Conversations: Practicing the Parts* (p.186)
  Graphic organizer for Personal Story (p.187)

Note: Make students put handouts and other materials in the appropriate section of their notebooks after each lesson.

1. Review homework.

2. Go over Personal Stories, discussing other options for behavior in the situation (with older students focus on consequences of actions – how one's actions affect others and oneself).

3. Talk about the purpose of the lesson (*to practice all the parts of a conversation*).

4. Tape a long sheet of paper to the wall. Have two children at a time stand facing each other in front of the paper; either trace their heads or use a light to make shadows and trace their silhouettes. Do this four times with four pairs of children. Now divide the cartoon strip by making boxes around each pair of heads with a thick black marker. Make conversation bubbles above each head. Below the heads, write one of the four parts of conversation in order. Take the strip down and let the children color it.

5. Put the strip back on the wall once it has been colored and fill in the bubbles. For the greeting, write "Hello" and "Hi"; for small talk, write "How was your day?" "It was fine. How was yours?" "Fine."; for the main topic, write "I wanted to talk to you about ..."; for the closing, write "Nice talking to you. Goodbye." "Bye."

6. Have pairs of children stand in front of the strip and role-play a conversation by going through each part. Tell them that the main topic can be (a) asking for a play date, (a) asking if the other child wants to play together at lunch, (c) talking about the content of a movie they saw or a book they read, etc.

7. Demonstrate different parts of a conversation with one of the children or another adult and ask the children to name a given part.

8. Hand out homework, including a blank graphic organizer.

9. Give each child a secret responsibility.

Social Skills Homework #24:
Conversations: Practicing the Parts

Dear Parents,

Today we practiced the parts of a conversation.

1. Write a personal story (use the graphic organizer) *with* your child about something that happens between sessions.

2. Please review the work in your child's notebook. Go over all rules for parts of a conversation.

3. Your child has a secret responsibility at home this week. The child is supposed to carry out this responsibility so well that by the end of the week you can guess what it is. Please send your guess in a note in the social skills notebook. Do not ask your child what the responsibility is. Let him/her feel that he/she is totally responsible.

Child's Homework

Please answer the following questions. Write your answers on a separate sheet of paper. Do this with one of your parents. (*Parents, remember, if your child has difficulty writing the responses, you may write them in.*)

1. Do your secret responsibility.

2. Practice the parts of a conversation with one of your parents.

3. Answer these questions:
   - Are there times when you shouldn't start small talk and you should get straight to the main point? If so, when?

   - When small talk is not appropriate, there are only three parts of conversation you will use. What are they?

Personal Story Organizer

What happened?

_____
_____
_____
_____

My Personal Story

Consequences?

_____
_____
_____
_____

What should you do next time?

_____
_____
_____
_____

Social Skills Lesson #25

MY BEHAVIOR AFFECTS OTHERS AND COMES BACK TO ME – #1

Goals:

To discuss how a person's behavior affects other people, how inappropriate behavior can make others feel and behave toward the person.

Materials

- blackboard and chalk
- loose-leaf paper
- markers
- Frog and Toad story, "The Dream," in *Frog and Toad Together* by Arnold Lobel (New York: Harper Collins Children's Books, 1979)
- copies of handouts and homework
  Handout A, *Cause-and-Effect Organizer Example* (p. 190)
  Handout B, *Frog and Toad Organizer* (p. 191)
  Social Skills Homework: *My Behavior Affects Others and Comes Back to Me – #1* (p.192)
  Graphic organizer for Personal Story (p. 193)

Note: Make sure students put handouts and other materials in the appropriate section of their notebooks after each lesson.

1. Review homework.

2. Go over Personal Stories, discussing other options for behavior in the situation (with older students focus on consequences of actions – how one's actions affect others and oneself).

3. Talk about the purpose of the lesson (*to understand that my behavior affects other people and inappropriate behavior can make others leave me/not be my friends*).

4. Discuss cause and effect using the graphic organizer in Handout A.

5. Read the Frog and Toad story.

6. Make a cause-and-effect graphic organizer for the children to copy based on the story (see Handout B). For example, in the organizer describe Toad's behavior and how it causes Frog to feel and how Toad is affected in the end.

7. Write out the lesson to be learned from the story and have the children copy.

MY BEHAVIOR AFFECTS OTHERS AND ME
- STOP
- THINK (I should treat other people the way that I want to be treated)
  - I should not yell; I should just say how I feel.
  - I should use "put-ups."
  - I should not tell people I am better than them.
  - (NOTE: Add specifics for the children in your group.)
- GO!

---

8. Hand out homework, including a blank graphic organizer.

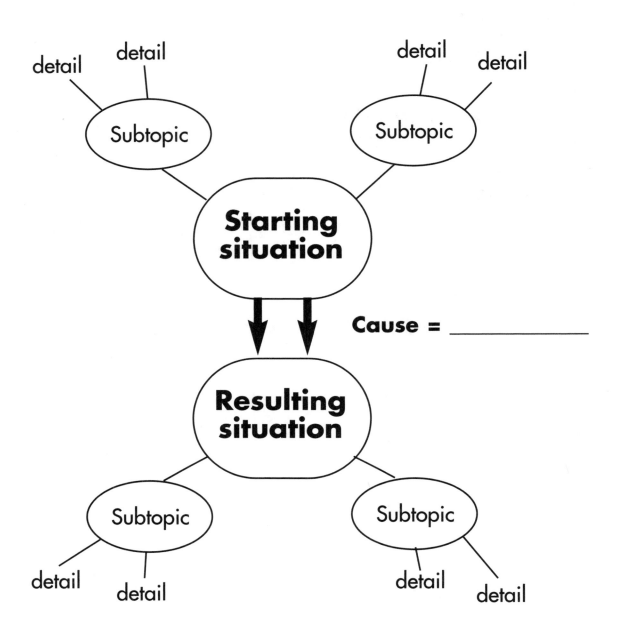

Handout B, Lesson #25:
Frog and Toad Organizer

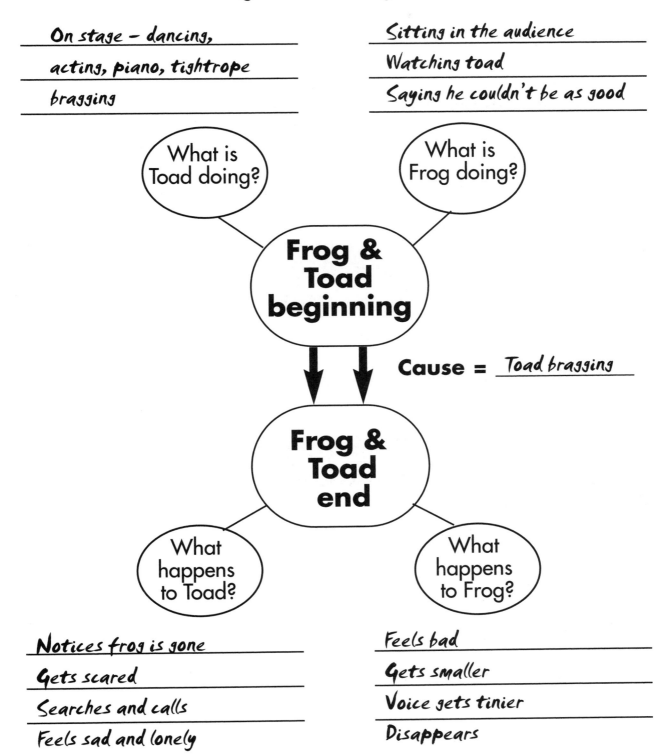

On stage – dancing, acting, piano, tightrope bragging

Sitting in the audience
Watching toad
Saying he couldn't be as good

What is Toad doing?

What is Frog doing?

Frog & Toad beginning

Cause = Toad bragging

Frog & Toad end

What happens to Toad?

What happens to Frog?

Notices frog is gone
Gets scared
Searches and calls
Feels sad and lonely

Feels bad
Gets smaller
Voice gets tinier
Disappears

Social Skills Homework #25:
MY BEHAVIOR AFFECTS OTHERS AND COMES BACK TO ME - #1

Dear Parents,

Today we learned about how a child's inappropriate behaviors can make others want to leave.

1. Write a Personal Story (use the graphic organizer) *with* your child about something that happens between sessions.

2. Please review the work in your child's notebook. Go over all rules.

3. Help your child recall a time when he/she did not think about how his/her behavior would affect other people's feelings, how the other people felt, and how this came back to affect your child. Discuss and write out the story with your child. Send the story to school in your child's social skills notebook.

Child's Homework

1. Tell two people about the story we read in this week's session. Use your graphic organizer to help you.

Personal Story Organizer

What happened?

_____
_____
_____
_____

My Personal Story

Consequences?

_____
_____
_____
_____

What should you do next time?

_____
_____
_____
_____

Social Skills Lesson #26

MY BEHAVIOR AFFECTS OTHERS AND COMES BACK TO ME – #2

Goals:

To reinforce the idea that our behavior affects others and how they feel about and behave towards us. To understand that some behaviors are inappropriate at times but appropriate at others. To discuss the ways people can tell that they made a mistake and recall what people should do if they make a mistake.

Materials

- blackboard and chalk
- loose-leaf paper
- markers
- book: *Norma Jean Jumping Bean* by J. Cole, illustrated by L. Munsinger (New York: Random House Children's Books, 2003)
- copies of handouts and homework
  Handout A1, *Empty Norma Jean Jumping Bean* (p. 196)
  Handout A2, *Sample Norma Jean Jumping Bean* (p. 197)
  Handout B1, *Empty Norma Jean Jumping Bean* (p. 198)
  Handout B2, *Sample Norma Jean Jumping Bean* (p. 199)
  Handout C, *My Behavior Affects Others and Me* (p. 200)
  Social Skills Homework: *My Behavior Affects Others and Comes Back to Me – #2* (p. 201)
  Graphic organizer for Personal Story (p. 202)

Note: Make sure students put handouts and other materials in the appropriate section of their notebooks after each lesson.

1. Review homework.

2. Go over Personal Stories, discussing other options for behavior in the situation (with older students focus on consequences of actions – how one's actions affect others and oneself).

3. Talk about the purpose of the lesson (*understanding how my behavior affects others' feelings about me and that some behaviors are inappropriate at times but appropriate at others*).

4. Read *Norma Jean Jumping Bean.*

5. Have the students fill in the cause-and-effect graphic organizer based on the first part of the story (see Handout A). Discuss Norma's behavior and how it causes her friends to feel. Also discuss how Norma is affected by the others' reaction.

6. Have the students fill in a second cause-and-effect graphic organizer based on the second part of the story (see Handout B). Discuss Norma's behavior when she starts jumping again at field day and how it causes her friends to feel. Also discuss how Norma is affected by her friends' reaction.

7. Write out the lessons to be learned from *Norma Jean Jumping Bean* and have the children copy.

BEHAVIOR CAN BE O.K. SOMETIMES AND NOT O.K. OTHER TIMES
- STOP
- THINK
  - Remember when a behavior is inappropriate, it may make people feel bad about you
  - Some behaviors are inappropriate sometimes and appropriate at others
- GO!
  - Use appropriate behaviors

---

8. Make a list (have the children copy): *WAYS I CAN TELL I HAVE MADE A MISTAKE* (people will tell me, people will get angry, people will leave).

9. Give older children Handout C, *My Behavior Affects Others and Me.*

10. Hand out homework, including a blank graphic organizer.

What does
Norma Jean
do at school?

_____
_____
_____
_____

What does
Norma Jean
do at home?

What does
Norma Jean
do at play?

_____
_____
_____
_____

_____
_____
_____
_____

**Norma Jean
beginning**

CAUSE: _____

_____

**Norma Jean
middle**

_____
_____
_____
_____

_____
_____
_____
_____

What
happened
at school?

What
happened
at play?

Handout A2, Lesson #26:

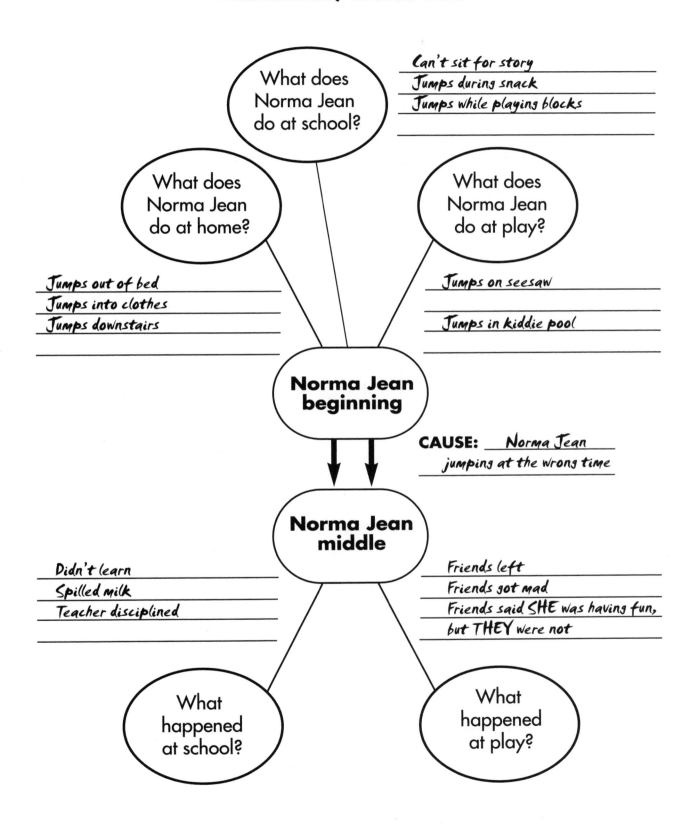

What does Norma Jean do at school?
- Can't sit for story
- Jumps during snack
- Jumps while playing blocks

What does Norma Jean do at home?
- Jumps out of bed
- Jumps into clothes
- Jumps downstairs

What does Norma Jean do at play?
- Jumps on seesaw
- Jumps in kiddie pool

Norma Jean beginning

CAUSE: Norma Jean jumping at the wrong time

Norma Jean middle

- Didn't learn
- Spilled milk
- Teacher disciplined

- Friends left
- Friends got mad
- Friends said SHE was having fun, but THEY were not

What happened at school?

What happened at play?

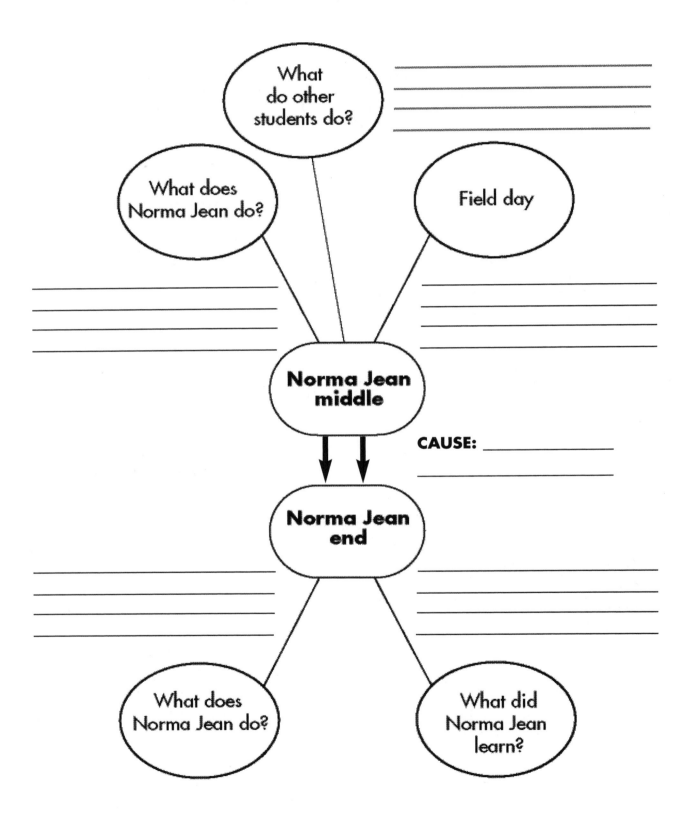

Handout B2, Lesson #26:

What
do other
students do?

Jump rope
Jump over puddles
Run & play in school year
Miss "old" Norma Jean

What does
Norma Jean do?

Field day

Does not jump at all

Feels sad

Other kids enter contests
Norma Jean jumps a little
Norma Jean doesn't enter

**Norma Jean
middle**

CAUSE: Norma Jean sees times
when it is OK to jump.

**Norma Jean
end**

Decides can jump at field day
Hurdles
Sack race
Jumps for joy

Jump rope

Jump rope

What does
Norma Jean do?

What did
Norma Jean
learn?

My Behavior Affects Others and Me

If I brag, I make others feel small ...

If I am mean, I make others angry and sad ...

If I am pushy, I make others feel upset and like they don't want to cooperate ...

If I am unpredictable, people are afraid and stay away ...
  ... and maybe they will disappear.

If I am kind, I make others feel happy and liked ...

If I cooperate appropriately, I make others feel happy, cared about, and strong ...
  ... and people feel good about me.

Social Skills Homework #26:
MY BEHAVIOR AFFECTS OTHERS AND COMES BACK TO ME – #2

Dear Parents,

Today we learned about behaviors that are appropriate at one time but not at others.

1. Write a Personal Story (use the graphic organizer) *with* your child about something that happens between sessions.

2. Please review the work in your child's notebook. Go over all rules.

3. Point out behaviors your child exhibits that are appropriate under some circumstances and not under others and discuss why.

Child's Homework

1. Name a behavior that is appropriate at one time but not appropriate at another time.

   _____

   _____

   _____

2. Tell two people about the Norma Jean story. Use your graphic organizer to help you. Tell how in the first part of the story Norma's behavior made others not like her. Which of Norma's behaviors was inappropriate at one time but appropriate at another?

Personal Story Organizer

What
happened?

_____
_____
_____
_____
_____

**My Personal
Story**

Consequences?

_____
_____
_____
_____
_____

What should
you do next
time?

_____
_____
_____
_____

Social Skills Lesson #27

REVIEW

Goal:

To review pull-out lessons #14 through 26.

Materials

- social skills notebooks
- social skills test (pp. 204-205)

1. Review homework.

2. Go over Personal Stories, discussing other options for behavior in the situation (with older students focus on consequences of actions – how one's actions affect others and oneself).

3. Talk about the purpose of the lesson (review all social skills lessons #14-26 and give test).

4. Ask all children the questions on the test.
   (Give the written test to older children for homework.)

Lesson #27
Social Skills Test #2

Name:_____

1. What are the four parts of a conversation?

    1.

    2.

    3.

    4.

2. What are the three things you can do to continue the main topic of a conversation?

    1.

    2.

    3.

3. When would it not be a good time to start small talk?

    _____

    _____

4. Write a topic sentence for the topic "grandparents."

    _____

    _____

5. List two things you should not do when you are angry.

   1.

   2.

6. What should you do when you are angry?

   _____

   _____

7. Who is responsible for your behavior?

   _____

   _____

8. Who should control other people's behavior?

   _____

   _____

9. What should the following parts of your body be doing when you are listening to someone:

   eyes _____

   ears _____

   brain _____

   head _____

S.O.S. Peer Mentoring

Overview

In the peer mentoring component of the S.O.S. program, selected typically developing children are trained and supervised in one session per week (run as a lunchtime or after-school club).

Goals

The goals of the peer mentoring program for the children with PDD and the mentors are as follows:
- To train same-age peers as play facilitators, mediators, recess and lunch buddies and social skills coaches for children with PDD.

- To have trained mentors engage children with PDD, cue appropriate social behavior, support personal goals, and mediate conflict.

Staff and Time Commitment

- **The S.O.S. social skills trainer/peer mentor supervisor** trains and supervises mentors.

- **The S.O.S. social skills trainer/peer mentor supervisor** observes on the playground as needed.

- **Classroom teachers** reinforce the program by reminding peer mentors of their scheduled day to mentor, by observing the children with PDD interact with their peer mentors and providing feedback to the social skills trainer/peer mentor supervisor, and by giving advice to peer mentors and children with PDD as needed.

- **Lunch/playground supervisors** support the program by observing the children with PDD interact with their peer mentors and providing feedback to the social skills teacher/peer mentor supervisor.

- **Parents of children with PDD** support the program by helping their children complete S.O.S. homework and by attending parent meetings held by the program supervisor. Parents of mentors support the program by talking with their children about mentoring, helping them problem solve, and by attending a meeting with the mentor supervisor. They also support the program by complying with the rules of confidentiality (see pages 209, 227).

Recruitment of Peer Mentors

Characteristics

Children selected as peer mentors must have strong social skills and be good listeners and good observers. They should be children who do not typically lay blame but rather seek out the reasons behind conflict and try to resolve differences in positive, constructive ways.

Peer mentoring is explained to the students during the S.O.S. classroom lessons as noted. The children must understand that mentoring is a privilege and a serious responsibility. They also should be told that there is not room for every child to be selected as a peer mentor, so only some of the students who volunteer will be selected.

Candidates for peer mentor may be identified in the following ways:
- Student volunteers
- Teacher nominations

After observing the candidates in their classrooms during the S.O.S. classroom lessons, the social skills trainer/mentor supervisor selects candidates who meet the stated criteria. Three to four peer mentors should be selected for each child with PDD in the program. The peer mentors and the children with PDD they are assigned to must be in the same grade.

Parents, teachers, the student, and the social skills trainer/mentor supervisor must agree that the child meets the stated criteria to be a peer mentor.

Parental Permission

Parental permission must be obtained for each mentor's participation. It must be clear to the parents in giving permission for their son or daughter to participate that the mentor is free to withdraw from the program at any time. In addition, if a mentor abuses his or her position with the child mentored or displays other seriously inappropriate behaviors, a meeting will be called with the mentor's parents to discuss and rectify the situation. It is important that the mentor be given an opportunity to replace his or her inappropriate behavior with appropriate behavior. However, sustained inappropriate behavior, especially toward the child to be mentored, will result in expulsion from the program.

Post-Recruitment Meeting with Parents

Once all peer mentors have been identified, an orientation meeting is held with the parents of the mentors to review the program and answer any questions (see page 227). This meeting will focus on what the mentors will be taught in the lessons, as well as behavioral expectations and rules of participation. In addition, the discussion should emphasize the necessity of maintaining the confidentiality of the mentees and their families. That is, parents must understand and agree that discussion of the mentees is allowed only in their home with their own children who are mentors. Public discussion of mentees will result in expulsion of mentors from the program. Parents are also reminded that the children must bring a loose-leaf binder to the first peer mentor training session.

SAMPLE PERMISSION LETTER FOR RECRUITING PEER MENTORS

(School Letterhead)

Our school district is implementing Dr. Michelle Dunn's S.O.S. (*Social Skills in Our Schools*) program to help children who have difficulty making friends and sustaining friendships. The children may be unaware of how to make friends, or inappropriate behaviors may get in their way.

An important part of the social skills intervention is a mentoring component. The other components are: social skills lessons taught to all children in the classroom and small-group pull-out social skills training sessions (one hour per week) for the children with social skills challenges. Your child has expressed an interest in being a peer mentor. I would like to provide some background information about what is involved.

Each peer mentor will be trained and supervised by an adult in the school to support and guide the social interactions of children who have weak social skills. Once trained, peer mentors will help the child to whom they are assigned during lunch and recess.

Each mentor is assigned to a specific child, but there will be more than one mentor for each child so that your son/daughter would only be responsible for mentoring, on average, once a week. Peer mentors are supervised on a weekly basis outside of class time. They will be taught about the social difficulties of their assigned child and will be given ways to help the child interact on the playground. They will report to the supervisor about how the work is going and any difficulties encountered.

If you agree to allow your child to be a peer mentor, please sign and return the permission slip below. By signing the permission slip, you are agreeing not only to allow your child to be a peer mentor but also to maintain the confidentiality of the child being mentored and his/her family.

You are free to withdraw your child from the S.O.S. peer mentoring program at any time. If you have any questions about the program, please contact _____ at _____.

Thank you for your interest and support,

_____
S.O.S. Signature of Supervisor

I give permission for my child _____ to participate in the S.O.S. program as a peer mentor. I understand that s/he will be trained and receive weekly supervision.

_____
Signature of parent

_____
Date

S.O.S. Peer Mentor Training

Overall Structure of Mentor Training and Supervision Sessions

- **Notebooks**

  All mentors must keep a notebook for lesson handouts and notes from the supervision sessions. Please note that names of the PDD children being mentored should NOT be written in the notebook.

- **Intervention Methods**

  - Direct teaching of rules for intervention.

  - Role-playing: Adults role-play correct and incorrect ways to mentor in various situations. The potential mentors practice by role-playing the correct way.

  Note: Adapt the following lessons to the developmental level of the children participating.

Lesson 1

WHAT DO PEER MENTORS DO?

Goals

- To discuss the role of peer mentors.
- To discuss how to help the students to be mentored get into games and conversations.

Materials

- blackboard and chalk
- loose-leaf paper
- copies of Handout A (page 215)

1. Explain how the children will use their peer mentoring notebooks. It is a place to write notes and keep handouts from the training and supervision sessions. Make sure they understand that they should not write the names of the children they mentor in their books.
2. Reiterate the rules of participation as peer mentors and their responsibility (see pages 17-19).
3. Explore the role of mentors.

Activities

1. Hand out copies of Handout A and have the children put it in their notebooks. Discuss the content of the sheet regarding the roles of mentors:

   #### Peer mentors are recess and lunch helpers:

   - *They help children get into conversations, games, etc.*
   - *They help children remember how to behave appropriately. They support students' personal goals.*
   - *They help solve conflicts.*

2. Tell the children that each of them will be assigned a specific child to help, but that three to four of them will be assigned to the same child. Emphasize that being a peer mentor is both a responsibility and a privilege. Tell the children that they were selected for the program because they have good social skills. (Remind them that seriously inappropriate behavior will result in a mentor being asked to leave the program.)

3. Discuss what typically happens on the playground during recess.
   - Discuss what it feels like to be left out. Talk about children they have noticed on the playground or during lunch who are usually on the outside. How do you think they feel? How might we help?
   - Make a list of the kinds of games kids play on the playground and another list of things kids typically talk about.
   - Talk about what the mentors themselves usually do to join games or conversations if they are not already involved in them.

4. Role-play some of the following situations:
   - Good time to join play (e.g., kids playing catch or tag)
   - Good time to join conversation (e.g., kids talking about a lesson you were in with them)
   - Inappropriate time to start play or conversation (e.g., children enter class and the teacher says it is time to sit down and get started)
   - Inappropriate time to try to get into a game (e.g., Checkers game already in progress)
   - Inappropriate time to start a conversation (e.g., ball game/running game starting up or in progress)

5. Discuss how you know if it's a good time or not to initiate an interaction.

6. Write out the rules for initiating and have the children copy them.

RULES FOR INITIATING

STOP, THINK (is it a good time to interrupt?) If yes,

GO!

(They explain what they are thinking to their assigned child)

- Make eye contact
- Have a friendly face
- Say "hi"
- THINK: Do you want to join the person? Is it a good time?
- THINK: Start a conversation, play, wait until later?
  (Some examples of utterances the children can use for initiating interaction are: "What are you doing?" "Can I play too?")

Handout A, Peer Mentoring

Peer mentors are recess and lunch helpers:

- They help kids get into conversations, games, etc.

- They help kids remember how to behave appropriately. They support personal goals.

- They help solve conflicts.

Lesson #2
PRACTICING WHAT PEER MENTORS DO

Goal:

To practice helping other kids get into games and conversations.

Materials

- blackboard and chalk
- loose-leaf paper

Activities

1. Review the rules for initiating from Peer Mentor Lesson #1 (page 214).

2. Tell the children that as mentors there are three ways they can help the child they are mentoring get into a game or conversation. Have them copy the following:

   Three Ways a Mentor Helps:
   - Tell the child what to do.
   - Model the behavior and tell the child to imitate.
   - Ask the child what she thinks she should do and encourage her to do the right thing.

3. Role-play some of the situations from Lesson #1 again, but this time have one child be a mentor and another play the role of the child being mentored.

   (Make sure the students understand that it is common for initiations during recess to be met with rejection and that they should reassure the children they work with not to take it personally and to keep trying.)

Lesson #3

STOP, THINK, GO

Goals:

- **To teach the mentors to stop and think before they decide what to do to help.**
- **To teach the mentors that it is important to help the students they mentor to remember to stop and think before they act.**

Materials

- blackboard and chalk
- paper stoplight
- loose-leaf paper
- tape recorder
- music tapes

Activities

1. Talk with the group about the topics you will be covering in the social skills pull-out sessions (learning social rules, practicing social rules, etc.). Tell them that one of the most important lessons is learning how to stop. Explain that there is a special way of stopping that their mentees have learned and that they are to use with their mentees when it is needed.

2. Have children copy the following from the blackboard:

   STOP   **"Don't do anything until you have a plan"**

   THINK   **"Think of a plan"**

   GO   **"Try the plan"**

3. Discuss what each step means.

4. Tell the students that the point of today's lesson is to understand the steps for learning appropriate behavior and to practice stopping. Read the "Jimmy Gets Too Silly" (page 64) and "Jimmy Gets Too Angry" (page 153) stories with the mentors. Talk about the consequences of failing to stop when necessary.

5. Write out the rules for how to stop on the board and have children copy them.

> **RULES FOR STOPPING**
> * Take a deep breath.
> * Count to 10 slowly.
> * Say to myself, "I can stop."

6. Have the children pretend to lose control in a variety of ways (anger, anxiety, etc.) and demonstrate for them how to get back in control.

Draw a "thermometer" on the blackboard. At the end of each activity, have the students indicate on the thermometer how "out of control they were." The higher the "mercury" on the thermometer, the more out of control the child felt. Help them to understand your perception. Was their perception the same as yours?

Practice situations where another child pretends to lose control and they cue that child with STOP (using the Rules for Stopping) and THINK. Tell the children that they are only to do this with the student assigned to them.

Lesson #4
MEDIATING CONFLICT

Goal:

To teach and rehearse the steps for mediating conflict.

Materials

- blackboard and chalk
- loose-leaf paper

Activities

1. Make a list of the kinds of conflicts children see at lunch and recess.

2. Go over and have children copy the steps for mediation as follows:
   a. Is there a problem?
   b. Do you want to solve it?
   c. Go to a quiet place.
   d. State the ground rules: we won't yell or be mean; we will listen and keep trying until the problem is solved.
   e. Each child tells his/her story.
   f. Children search for solutions.
   g. Children select solution.
   h. Mediation closed.

3. Ask students to suggest examples.

4. Role-play mediations using examples of conflicts provided by the children.

Lesson #5
UNDERSTANDING CONTINGENCY PLANS

Goal:

To learn contingency plans for difficult situations that may occur with the children they mentor.

Materials

- blackboard and chalk
- loose-leaf paper

Activities

1. Explain to the children that adults are there to back up their efforts. For example, you, their supervisor, will be there during lunch and recess when they first implement the S.O.S. program. When you are no longer there, the playground supervisors will be there. They will be aware of what the peer mentors are doing and will help when necessary.

2. Discuss and develop plans for the following common problems and any others you and the students come up with:

   - *One child agrees to play or to mediation but the other doesn't*
     (Solution: The mentor stops playing or mediation with the child who refuses and goes over to play with the child who is willing to interact. The mentor later reports back to the mentor supervisor to get advice.)

   - *Children walk away and refuse to continue playing or complete mediation*
     (Solution: The mentor stops playing or mediation, and later reports back to the mentor supervisor to get advice.)

   - *Assigned children run away from mentors*
     (Solution: The mentored child might be more responsive and less anxious if prepared in advance for what will happen on the playground. The mentor can make a plan for the playground with the mentee during lunch. It is important that the mentee knows how to play the suggested game. Another way to engage the mentee is to ask what she wants to play and then to play that game.)

- *Arguments or name-calling start*
  (Solution: The mentor tells the lunch supervisor.)

- *Verbal or physical fights erupt*
  (Solution: The mentor tells the lunch supervisor.)

- *The mentor is teased*
  (Solution: The mentor walks away, and later reports back to the mentor supervisor to get advice.)

3. Make it clear to the mentors that physical aggression is NEVER allowed and that if they encounter it, they must quickly get an adult to help.

4. Role-play the situations in Step #2.

Lesson #6

WHO ARE THE CHILDREN WE WILL HELP?

Goal:

Getting ready to start.

Materials

- blackboard and chalk
- loose-leaf paper
- list of PPD students' names

Activities

1. Give out names of children to be helped. Discuss the difficulties each child has. Review the personal goal of each child to be helped.

2. Tell the mentors that the best way to start helping their assigned child is simply to invite the child into their game or conversation.

3. Tell the mentors that when their assigned child is having trouble socially, they are to tell or show the child the appropriate thing to do.

4. Discuss appropriate ways to cue the children they mentor:
   - **No physical cueing** (mentors are not to touch or physically lead the children they mentor)
   - **Visual cueing** (it is easier for the children to learn through demonstration than through telling)
   - **O.K. to be directive at first** (tell the students to quietly show and tell the mentee exactly what to do. When the child gets better at being with other children on the playground, let her try playing with others first and help if the child starts having trouble.)

5. Review all lessons.

6. Role-play:
   - Helping to Initiate
   - Helping to Stop and Decide
   - Mediating a Conflict
   - Contingency Plans

Lesson #7

THE FIRST MEETING

Have a pizza or ice cream party with the mentors and the children with PDD before the mentors start their work during lunch and on the playground.

Note: The peer mentor supervisor must observe the first mentoring session on the playground. If problems are reported (e.g., the mentee consistently rejects the mentors, the mentor feels uncertain of his or her interaction with the mentee) at any time during the year in supervision, the mentor supervisor should follow up with further observation.

Lessons #8-21

MENTOR SUPERVISION

1. All subsequent sessions with the mentors include abbreviated versions of the lessons that are given in the pull-out sessions for the children with social skills needs – the children they are mentoring. This allows the mentors to facilitate and reinforce all new social skills the children have learned in their pull-out sessions.

   The following is a suggested schedule for teaching the peer mentors the concepts covered in the pull-out sessions:
   8. Pull-out lessons #3 & 4 (pp. 77-90)
   9. Pull-out lesson #5 (pp. 91-96)
   10. Pull-out lesson #6 & 7 (pp. 97-104)
   11. Pull-out lesson #10 (pp. 114-117)
   12. Pull-out lesson #11 & 12 (pp. 118-125)
   13. Pull-out lesson #14 & 15 (pp. 129-140)
   14. Pull-out lesson #17 &18 (pp. 145-158)
   15. Pull-out lesson #19 (pp. 159-163)
   16. Pull-out lesson #20 (pp. 164-169)
   17. Pull-out lessons #20 & 21 (pp. 164-174)
   18. Pull-out lessons #22 & 23 (pp. 175-183)
   19. Pull-out lesson #24 (pp. 184-187)
   20. Pull-out lesson #25 (pp. 188-193)
   21. Pull-out lesson #26 (pp. 194-202)

2. In addition, each week during supervision, mentors are asked to describe their interactions with the children during lunch and on the playground. Any questions are answered. When appropriate, role-playing occurs to clarify appropriate mentor responses to situations that have occurred.

   As the school year progresses, the mentors should help bring their assigned children not only into their own games but also into other children's games. In addition, the mentors should become less directive as their assigned children gain social competence, letting the mentees try out their new social skills, helping and supporting as needed instead of telling the mentees what to do.

Parent Training
225

Goals

1. A meeting at the beginning of the school year for **parents of mentors** orients them to the S.O.S. program and their children's responsibilities as mentors. The meeting also reviews informed consent and issues of confidentiality.

2. Separate parent meetings are held to train **parents of children with PDD** in the goals and methods used in the S.O.S. program so that they can support generalization of social skills by completing homework and reinforcing social skills rules with their children.

   These meetings also offer a forum where parents can discuss and get advice concerning their children.

Staff and Time Commitment

1. The **mentor supervisor** holds one meeting with the parents of the mentors in the fall once mentors have been selected.

2. The certified **S.O.S. supervisor** meets with the parents of the children with PDD on a bi-monthly basis during the school year (five times).

Mentor Parents' Meeting

(*run by mentor supervisor*)

Sample Agenda

1. Give the parents an overview of the S.O.S. program.

2. Describe the characteristics of children who are selected to serve as mentors.

3. Discuss peer mentor responsibilities.

4. Describe peer mentor training and supervision (including the contents of the lessons). Point out that the students will need a 1-1/2 inch loose-leaf binder for keeping handouts and other materials.

5. Review informed consent forms (see page 210) and make sure that you have a signed form for each mentor.

6. Discuss the importance of maintaining confidentiality for the children being mentored and their families. Tell the parents to encourage their children to talk with them and the peer mentor supervisor about the children they mentor, if necessary. Discourage them from talking with other children in the class except to invite them to interact with the children they are mentoring.

   Note: The mentee's diagnosis is NEVER discussed, only the weakness in social skills.

Meetings for Parents of Children with PDD

(run by certified S.O.S. program supervisor)

Sample Agenda

Meeting 1

Overview of the S.O.S. program
- explain that if the parents prefer, social skills pull-out lessons may be offered without mentoring
- point out that mentoring *will not* be offered unless the child is participating in the pull-out lessons (i.e., it is difficult for the children to be responsive to social initiations by their peers unless they have already acquired some social skills and strategies)

Discussion of the following:
- format of social skills notebook (one divider; classwork in section 1 and homework in section 2)
- the need for parents to review weekly lessons and reinforce social rules through homework and practice (stress that consistency is critical to progress)
- importance of presenting material visually
- what the child with PDD will be taught with regard to emotional modulation (review the stopping strategy, page 63). Explain that it is important to practice the strategy out of the heat of the moment; that is, when the child is not completely out of control or in major distress, so that the child will be able to implement the strategy later when cued while in distress
- format for learning social rules (STOP, THINK, GO) (see pages 62-63, 71-72)
- Personal Stories – explain how to use the graphic organizers (pages 68 and 70) to recount Personal Stories. Parents have to fill in the graphic organizer with their child but they do not have to write the story out in prose; ask parents to alternate stories over the sessions between stories about appropriate social behaviors and stories about inappropriate behaviors displayed by the child; encourage parents to help their child with PDD come up with stories about his or her successes in using social rules taught in the pull-out sessions
- Issues of confidentiality. Be clear that their child's diagnosis will not be given to mentors, mentors' parents or anyone else except other school staff, or with their express written permission.

Meeting 2

Discussion of the following:
- personal goals: Explain that in addition to learning social rules in pull-out sessions, the children will be working on a personal goal. The goal will be identified by the social skills teacher in collaboration with the parents and the classroom teacher; it will address a typical or persistent social/behavioral problem the child encounters.
- responsibility: Discuss the idea that it is important for children to take responsibility for their work and progress to the extent that they can. Parents can engender a sense of responsibility in their children by helping them to be responsible for their belongings and

for contributing to their family (e.g., having a simple chore). Talk about the "secret responsibility" (pages 146, 148).

- assertiveness (teach the parents the May Booster Lesson on pages 51-54).
- how to best set up a play date/time. Parents will need support in providing direct instruction to their child in how to play and interact reciprocally, including how to share, how to attend to and understand the other child's needs and feelings, how to converse, and how to resolve conflicts. First play dates must be short, highly structured, and parent supported. Prior to the play date, it is important to find out what the other child enjoys doing and eating for snack. The parent can do this, or if the child with PDD has the skills to have this kind of conversation over the phone, he can call and ask. If the guest likes a game that is not familiar to the child with PDD, it is helpful to practice the game in a fun way prior to the play date. The play date should be planned with time for the guest to play his/her game, time for the host child to play his/her game, time for a snack, and time for a collaborative project. Knowing and accepting the schedule and time limits in advance can help the child with PDD to transition smoothly and have a good time at the play date. Even for older children with PDD, the activities should not stress conversational skill. A movie or bowling works well, with a little time for conversation over a snack. *The biggest mistakes in beginning play dates are to provide too little supervision and to let the play date go on for too long.* It is important to warn the child with PDD prior to each transition, and it is best to avoid over-stimulating activities at a play date until the child with PDD has good ability to stop.

Meeting 3

Discussion of the following:
- use of the description graphic organizer for developing language for understanding concepts and improving conversation (pull-out lesson # 20)
- conversation game: teach parents the game below and ask them to start playing it with their children following pull-out lesson #23

"The Conversation Game"

Game 1: "Keep It Going"

1. Make a set of index cards with a single topic written on each (e.g., sports, school, recess, my last trip with my family).

2. Make a stack of 21 cards, 7 of which say "ask a question," 7 say "make a comment," and 7 say "add information."

3. Put the two stacks of cards face down on the table.

   Practice: Have the players each trace one of their hands onto a piece of paper. Then have each select a topic card. On the traced hand the child should write a topic sentence on the main part of the hand and then a detail pertaining to the topic on each finger.

Play: Player #1 chooses a topic card. The other players each choose a card from the other pile. Player #1 generates a topic sentence about the topic selected and then five detail sentences. After Player #1 is finished, each child in the game does what his or her card says in turn. When everyone's turn is over, Player #2 selects a topic card and play continues as above.

Game 2: "Conversation Investigation"

The goal of this game is to develop the ability to ask questions that are contingent on what was said by a conversational partner.

1. Begin to talk about a topic and end after a couple of sentences with a statement with missing information. For example, "After school today I went to the park. It was such a beautiful day to sit on the bench and read. While I was there I saw something amazing."

2. Encourage the child to ask a question to get the missing information (e.g., "What did you see?").

As the kids get better at this, the missing information should be in the middle of the adult's sentences. For example, "I went on vacation last week. I went to my favorite place. I had a chance to relax and go swimming. It was so much fun." In this case the child should ask, "Where did you go?" Once the child can do this, encourage the child to ask a follow-up question that is contingent on the response received from the adult to the first question.

Meetings 4, 5

Group counseling sessions. There is no set agenda for these meetings. Parents are encouraged to ask specific questions about their child's behavior and about the S.O.S. program to get advice from the program supervisor about how to intervene. Parents are also encouraged to provide feedback regarding how their child is doing in the program. This helps establish new personal goals for the child.

Appendix

Rules

RULE FOR STOPPING
- Take a deep breath.
- Count to 10 slowly.
- Say to myself, "I can stop."

RULES FOR INTERRUPTING APPROPRIATELY
- STOP
- THINK (What is the appropriate way to interrupt? Is it a good time to interrupt?) If yes,
- GO!

Get the person's attention *(Say, "excuse me"; stand where the person can see you and look at him or her. When the person looks at you say "excuse me.")*

Say you are sorry for interrupting

Tell why you are interrupting

RULES FOR GREETINGS
- STOP
- THINK (Is this person familiar? How do I greet appropriately?)
- GO
  - Make eye contact.
  - Have a friendly face.
  - Say hi, or hello," or "good to see you." (<u>with the person's name if you know it</u>)

RULES FOR CLOSINGS
- STOP
- THINK (Is this person familiar? How do I greet appropriately?)
- GO
  - Make eye contact.
  - Have a friendly face.
  - Say "Good-bye" or "see you later." (<u>with the person's name if you know it</u>)

RULES FOR INITIATING AN INTERACTION

- STOP
- THINK (is it a good time to initiate an interaction?) If yes,
- GO!
  - Make eye contact
  - Have a friendly face
  - Say hi (If you know the person, say his name; if you don't know the person, introduce yourself. Say, "My name is_____; what's yours?")
  - THINK: What is the person doing? Do I want to join the person? Is it a good time?
  - THINK: Should I start a conversation, play with the person, or wait until later?
  - GO (Say, "What are you doing?"; "Can I join you?" "Can I play too?")

(For older children, also address initiation on the telephone. Use play telephones as props.)

RULES FOR ASKING FOR HELP

- STOP
- THINK (do I need help or should I keep trying myself?)
  - If you really need help,
- GO!
  - Interrupt appropriately
  - Clearly say what you need help with
  - Listen
  - If you do not understand, patiently ask questions
  - Say thank you

RULES FOR GIVING HELP

- STOP
- THINK (Did the person ask for help or did the person say YES when I asked, "Can I help you?")
- GO!
  - Listen to what the person needs.
  - If you do not understand, patiently ask questions.
  - Help if you can OR find someone who can help.

RULES FOR STAYING IN A GAME
DO

- Let others into your game
- Follow the rules
- Win or lose – be a good sport
- Compliment other kids ("That was great!")
- Share and take turns ("Would you like a turn?"; "Your turn"; "What do you want to play?")
- Play safe – if it gets too rough, walk away

DON'T

- Cry or whine
- Try to take control
- Push, hit
- Disrupt (wreck) the game

RULES FOR JOINING IN (IF YOU ARE READY)
DO

- Ask "Can I play?"
- Ask "What can I do?"
- Make sure you know the rules of the game
- Suggest what you can do in the group
- Make a plan with someone ahead of time
- Say something nice

DON'T

- Push, hit
- Brag
- Disagree with the group
- Just walk around
- Control the game
- Disrupt (wreck) the game
- Only talk about you
- Fool around

RULES FOR BECOMING A GOOD FRIEND

- Give compliments ("Good job," "Great idea," or when someone is upset, "It's O.K.," etc.)
- Smile
- Be helpful
- Take turns – let your friends have their way sometimes

RULES FOR EYE CONTACT AND BODY POSITION

- STOP
- THINK (shouldn't I make eye contact and turn to the person?)
- GO!
  When you are talking to someone or the person is talking to you:
  - Turn your body toward the person
  - Look at the other person's eyes
  - Look most of the time but don't stare

RULES FOR HOW CLOSE I SHOULD GET
- STOP
- THINK (am I too close or too far away from the other person?)
- GO!
    - Stay one arm's length away

RULES FOR VOLUME OF VOICE
- STOP, THINK (what volume should I use?)
- GO!
    - Sometimes you need to speak louder than normal and sometimes more quietly
    - Make sure the person you are talking to can hear you
    - BUT do not disturb others

RULES FOR LISTENING
- STOP
- THINK (what should my body and brain be doing while I listen?)
- GO!
    - Eyes look
    - Body faces person
    - Head nods
    - Ears hear what is being said
    - Brain thinks about what person is talking about
    - Mouth is quiet or says, "Uh huh"

"TWO-QUESTION RULE"
- STOP, THINK (I hear a question; what question can I ask?)
- GO!
    - When someone asks a question, answer it
    - Then ask a similar question
    - Wait for a response
    - TAKE TURNS

RULES FOR RESPONSIBILITY

- STOP, THINK (what is the responsible thing to do?)
- GO!
  - I HAVE THE POWER to control ME
  - I **do not** control others
  - Other people (my parents and teachers) are my helpers; they tell me the rules
  - I need to make good choices to do the right things according to the rules
  - If I do the right thing, people will feel good about me and like me

RULES ABOUT MISTAKES

- STOP (remind the kids that this is the hardest time to stop)
- THINK ("what should I do when I make a mistake?")
  - I can stop in the middle of making a mistake or losing control
  - I can apologize in the middle of a mistake ("Oops, I lost my head") or after I have made a mistake
  - I can say what I am sorry for ("I'm sorry for_____")
  - I can say what I will do differently next time. ("Next time I will _____")
- GO!
  - Keep stopping
  - Apologize

RULES FOR TALKING ABOUT TOPICS

- STOP
- THINK
  - What will I say?
  - I will talk about a main topic and then subtopics
- GO!
  - Start with a topic sentence about the main topic
  - Use a topic sentence for your first subtopic
  - Tell the details about your first subtopic
  - Talk about your other subtopics; always start with a topic sentence

RULES ABOUT WHAT TO DO FIRST IN A NEW SITUATION

- STOP
- THINK (What should I do first?)
  - Find the main topic
  - Is it a good time to start playing or talking with the others?
  - If YES,
- GO!
  - play or talk about the same topic as the other people
  - stick to the topic

RULES FOR CONTINUING ON A TOPIC IN CONVERSATION – #1

- STOP
- THINK (what is the topic?)
- GO!
  - Stick to the topic
  - Ask questions

RULES FOR CONTINUING ON A TOPIC IN CONVERSATION – #2

- STOP
- THINK (what is the topic?)
- GO!
  - Stick to the topic
  - Ask questions
  - Make comments
  - Add information

MY BEHAVIOR AFFECTS OTHERS AND ME

- STOP
- THINK (I should treat other people the way that I want to be treated)
  - I should not yell; I should just say how I feel.
  - I should use "put-ups."
  - I should not tell people I am better than them.
  - (NOTE: Add specifics for the children in your group.)
- GO!

BEHAVIOR CAN BE O.K. SOMETIMES AND NOT O.K. OTHER TIMES

- STOP
- THINK
  - Remember when a behavior is inappropriate, it may make people feel bad about you
  - Some behaviors are inappropriate sometimes and appropriate at others
- GO!
  - Use appropriate behaviors

OTHER SOCIAL SKILLS RESOURCES PUBLISHED BY AAPC

Asperger Syndrome and Difficult Moments: Practical Solutions for Tantrums, Rage, and Meltdowns; NEW EXPANDED EDITION
Brenda Smith Myles and Jack Southwick
Difficult Moments for Children and Youth with Autism Spectrum Disorders – DVD *Brenda Smith Myles*

When My Autism Gets Too Big!
A Relaxation Book for Children with Autism Spectrum Disorders
Kari Dunn Buron

Perfect Targets: Asperger Syndrome and Bullying; Practical Solutions for Surviving the Social World
Rebekah Heinrichs

The Incredible 5-Point Scale – Assisting Students with Autism Spectrum Disorders in Understanding Social Interactions and Controlling Their Emotional Responses
Kari Dunn Buron and Mitzi Curtis

Let's Talk Emotions: Helping Children with Social Cognitive Deficits, Including AS, HFA, and NVLD, Learn to Understand and Express Empathy and Emotions
Teresa A. Cardon

Social Skills Training for Children and Adolescents with Asperger Syndrome and Social-Communication Problems
Jed E. Baker

Joining In! A Program for Teaching Social Skills – Video
Created by: Linda Murdock and Guru Shabad Khalsa

Space Travelers: An Interactive Program for Developing Social Understanding, Social Competence and Social Skills for Students with Asperger Syndrome, Autism and Other Social Cognitive Challenges;
teacher and student guides
M. A. Carter and J. Santomauro

Peer Play and the Autism Spectrum – The Art of Guiding Children's Socialization and Imagination
Pamela J. Wolfberg

Super Skills: A Social Skills Group Program for Children with Asperger Syndrome, High-Functioning Autism and Related Challenges
Judith Coucouvanis

For further information or to place an order, please call **913-897-1004** or visit our website at **www.asperger.net**

Autism Asperger Publishing Company